THE INDIA-ISRAEL STRATEGIC PARTNERSHIP

Contours, Opportunities and Challenges

THE INDIA-ISRAEL STRATEGIC PARTNERSHIP

Contours, Opportunities and Challenges

S Samuel C Rajiv

MANOHAR PARRIKAR INSTITUTE FOR DEFENCE STUDIES AND ANALYSES

PENTAGON PRESS LLP

First published in 2023 by

PENTAGON PRESS LLP
206, Peacock Lane, Shahpur Jat
New Delhi-110049, India
Contact: 011-64706243

Typeset in AGaramond, 11.5 Point
Printed by Aegean Offset Printers, Greater Noida, U.P.

ISBN: 978-93-90095-70-4 (HB)

www.pentagonpress.in

Dedicated To My Wife
Esther Prabha Eladi

Contents

*

Chapter Tables

Appendix Tables

ACKNOWLEDGEMENTS

An Israeli government scholarship allowed me to spend time at the BESA Center for Strategic Studies in 2005-06. Since then, I have been a student of India-Israel relations. This book is an effort to capture the broad elements of the India-Israel bilateral relationship and the momentous changes they have undergone, in the past eight years. It builds on my Monograph, published in June 2022, which examined defence and security cooperation between the two countries.

Since my time at BESA, and now helming the Jerusalem Institute for Strategy and Security (JISS), Prof Efraim Inbar has been a kind mentor, to whom I am extremely grateful. I am grateful to the leadership at the Manohar Parrikar Institute for Defence Studies and Analyses (MP-IDSA) over the years, and Director General, Amb. Sujan R. Chinoy, for giving me opportunities to pursue my interest on the subject. I want to thank Shri Vivek Kaushik, Associate Editor, MP-IDSA, for his constant support and help in the publication process. Lastly, I want to thank the two anonymous Referees for their incisive comments which helped in improving the manuscript. Any errors are solely mine.

September 2022 **S Samuel C Rajiv**

1

INTRODUCTION

India-Israel relations took on a new dimension after Prime Minister Narendra Modi's visit to Jerusalem in July 2017. Bilateral relations are on a strong footing, with strengthened cooperation in the defence sector, apart from robust people-to-people links. Israel, for instance, accounted for nearly 15 per cent of foreign tourist arrivals (FTA) from West Asia during 2017-21, at more than 200,000 visitors cumulatively for that period.[1] India-Israel bilateral trade, from around US$ 500 million in 1995, peaked to around US$ 6.7 billion in 2011-12 but dropped to US$ 4.6 billion in 2020-21, in the wake of the pandemic. In 2021-22, bilateral trade increased to US$ 6897.42 million, a growth of nearly 50 per cent. The bilateral trade, though, is more often described as made up of 'diamonds and defence', as these components are the defining characteristics of the relationship. Trade in HS Classification code 71, relating to natural or cultured pearls and/or precious stones, for instance, during the last five years accounted for 36.7 per cent of total trade (US$ 9491.7 million out of a total cumulative trade of US$ 25,824 million during this period).[2]

As for the volume of defence trade, A.K. Antony, the then Defence Minister, informed the Upper House of Parliament (Rajya Sabha) in May 2007 that 'defence purchases' from Israel during 2002-2007 were over $5 billion.[3] Prior to this, in August 2005, Deputy Defence Minister B.K. Handique told the Rajya Sabha that 'the total value of the purchase contracts' with Israel during

2002-2005, for the purchase of 'military hardware, equipment and ammunition', was Rs. 11,882.54 crores.'[4] These amount to, perhaps, the two occasions when the Government of India informed the Parliament of the financial value of India-Israel defence cooperation.

In recent times, as during 2016-20, India accounted for 43 per cent of Israel's total arms exports, with Azerbaijan a distant second, accounting for 17 per cent.[5] Israel was the eighth-largest arms exporter globally during this period, accounting for 3 per cent of global arms exports, after the US, Russia, France, Germany, China, the United Kingdom and Spain. During 2017-21, India's share in Israel's global exports fell to 37 per cent, followed by Azerbaijan (13 per cent) and Vietnam (11 per cent), respectively.[6] Missiles and sensors overwhelmingly make up the bulk of defence exports from Israel. Since 2000, for instance, Israel has exported more than $13 billion worth of defence equipment, as per the Stockholm Peace Research Institute (SIPRI) Trend Indicator Values (TIVs). Out of these, missiles and sensors make up 58 per cent of the volume.[7]

Russia, meanwhile, was India's biggest arms supplier during 2017-21, accounting for 46 per cent of the country's imports.[8] During the previous five year period, 2012-16, India's arms imports from Russia stood at nearly 70 per cent of its total arms imports.[9] France (18 per cent) and Israel (13 per cent), other than Russia, made up the top three arms suppliers to India during 2016-20.[10] While India imported 18 per cent of its arms from France during this period, French exports to India accounted for 21 per cent of that country's total arms exports, ahead of Egypt and Qatar, at 20 and 18 per cent, respectively.[11] During 2017-21, French arms exports to India increased dramatically, accounting for 27 per cent of India's total imports, with the United States accounting for 12 per cent of India's arms imports, displacing Israel at the third position.[12]

Strengthened Partnership Post-2014

Prior to 2014, India's relations with Israel in particular and its approach towards the West Asian region in general, has been characterized as a 'fine balance', 'the delicate balance', and 'straddling fault lines'.[13] In the September 10, 2003 Delhi Statement on Friendship and Cooperation, signed when Prime Minister

Ariel Sharon visited India—the first ever visit by an Israeli Prime Minister—India and Israel had pledged to enhance the frequency of political and business interactions.[14]

While there was significant political traffic, with cabinet ministers and state chief ministers visiting Israel prior to 2017, high-level political interaction was missing. The term 'strategic partner' was also conspicuously absent in major bilateral documents like the September 2003 Joint Statement. Senior Indian cabinet ministers on their part, highlighted the need to not advertise their close defence and security relationship.

To be sure, India's high-level political interactions not just with Israel, but with other significant countries in West Asia like Saudi Arabia and Iran, were infrequent prior to 2014. India's West Asia policy, wading through the regional geopolitical hotspots though, continued to expand the scope for the pursuit of its national interests. India, for instance, engaged multiple regional players, even if these countries had inimical or non-existent relations bilaterally between themselves.

The Modi government built on the foundations of the robust India-Israel defence and security engagement. Prime Minister Modi assumed office in mid-2014, in the wake of the significant electoral victory achieved by the Bharatiya Janata Party (BJP)-led coalition. The BJP has been at the forefront of advocating stronger ties between India and Israel and its leaders have repeatedly expressed appreciation for Israel's muscular counter-terrorism and national security policies. Earlier in May 2006, as Chief Minister of Gujarat, Modi paid a successful visit to Israel, to attend a conference on agriculture technology.

Prime Minister Modi met Prime Minister Benjamin Netanyahu on the sidelines of the United Nations General Assembly (UNGA) in New York on September 28, 2014, the only second occasion when the Prime Ministers of India and Israel had met in the preceding eleven years. Netanyahu extended an invitation to Modi to visit Israel during this New York meeting. External Affairs Minister Sushma Swaraj in May 2015 – at a press briefing to highlight the achievements of the Modi government after a year in office, formally indicated that the Prime Minister would visit Israel, even though no specific dates had been agreed upon.[15]

Modi's meeting at the UNGA with Netanyahu was in the aftermath of 'Operation Protective Edge', the Israeli military action in the Gaza Strip, which began in July 2014. There was an unprecedented demand from the opposition in the Indian parliament for resolution critical of Israeli military action. The Government initially even refused to accept the demand for a discussion, with Swaraj stating that the 'subject refers discourteously to a friendly foreign country'.[16]

The discussion in the Rajya Sabha (Upper House), however, did eventually take place on July 21, 2014. During the discussion, the BJP Members of Parliament opposed demands from the opposition for a resolution critical of Israeli actions.[17] To the demands by the members of the Left parties that India should stop arms purchases from Israel, Foreign Minister Sushma Swaraj asked them why they had not raised a similar demand in 2008 or 2012 (probably referring to Israel's prior large-scale military actions 'Cast Lead' and 'Pillar of Defence').

Given the Modi government's spirited rebuttal of the opposition demands—coupled with the oft-expressed support for Israeli national security policies by BJP leaders, the opposition alleged that the Government was moving away from India's longstanding policy vis-a-vis their support to the Palestinians. While the Government rubbished the charges, reports in the media subsequently also speculated about the possibility of 'tectonic shift' in India's voting patterns as regards Israel-related resolutions at international fora under the Modi government.[18]

In the aftermath of Operation Protective Edge (the 2014 Israeli military operation in Gaza), President Pranab Mukherjee visited Israel and Palestine in October 2015. A series of MoUs relating to cooperation between the educational institutions of both countries were agreed upon. In February of that year, Israeli Defence Minister Moshe Yaalon visited Bengaluru (for Aero India 2015) and New Delhi. This was the first ever visit by an Israeli Defence Minister to India. It is noteworthy that no Indian Defence Minister has yet visited Israel. Foreign Minister Sushma Swaraj visited both Jerusalem and Ramallah in January 2016.

During Prime Minister Modi's July 2017 historic visit, the bilateral relationship was formally termed as a 'Strategic Partnership'.[19] Cooperation in the agriculture sector was strengthened, with the three-year Work Plan in Agriculture extended till 2020 (which has since been extended further), and the India-Israel Industrial R&D and Innovation Fund (I4F) was set up. Both sides pledged to invest $40 million in this Fund over five years ($4 million per year by each country) to promote joint R&D projects. The first round of project winners were announced in July 2018. These and subsequent successful project proposals related to novel treatments for glaucoma, as well as fields as diverse as agriculture, energy, water and Information and Communication Technology (ICT).

In the defence sector, joint development of products, including transfer of technology (ToT), was stressed, in the light of India's 'Make in India' initiative. Both sides agreed on a Framework for Cooperation in the Area of Cyber Security. Space cooperation was strengthened, with the Indian Space Research Organisation (ISRO) and the Israel Space Agency (ISA) signing agreements on projects relating to atomic clocks, geo-synchronous earth orbit (GEO)-low earth orbit (LEO) optical links and electric propulsion for small satellites.

While Prime Minister Modi visited Ramallah in a 'stand-alone' visit eight months later in February 2018, analysts found it significant that he did not go to Palestine during his path-breaking Israel visit. India's Israel policy, therefore, was termed as being 'de-hyphenated' from India's policy positions vis-à-vis Palestine.[20] During Prime Minister Netanyahu's January 2018 visit, a MoU on cooperation in the energy sector, was agreed upon. Both countries committed to explore opportunities in third countries – on aspects like agriculture, education, health care, solar energy and water, among others.[21] Both sides emphasized on the need for sustainable and long-term cooperation in the defence sector. The two Prime Ministers visited an innovation hub, the International Centre for Entrepreneurship and Technology, iCreate, in Ahmedabad. This hub was established in 2012 by the Gujarat government to foster innovation.

External Affairs Minister (EAM) S. Jaishankar's October 2021 visit—only the fourth foreign ministerial visit to Israel after the establishment of full diplomatic ties in 1992—showcased the intent of both countries to further strengthen the relationship which entered its fourth decade in January 2022, with emphasis on sustainability and 'Green' growth. A significant development that came out of the EAM's visit was the decision to resume discussions on a Free Trade Agreement (FTA) and complete the negotiations by 2022.[22]

As seen in the sections above, India-Israel relations have traversed a dynamic path. With the re-established intent to finish negotiations on an FTA—as mutually agreed during EAM Jaishankar's October 2021 visit, bilateral trade can be expected to grow from the current levels of around $5 billion. Defence cooperation, meanwhile, continues to be the strongest pillar of the relationship. The next chapter examines the defence cooperation between India and Israel in its varied dimensions.

NOTES

1. Ministry of Tourism, Government of India, 'India Tourism Statistics 2022', at https://tourism.gov.in/sites/default/files/2022-09/India%20Tourism%20Statistics%202022%20%28English%29_0.pdf (Accessed October 20, 2022).
2. Ministry of Commerce and Industry, 'Export Import Data Bank', at https://tradestat.commerce.gov.in/eidb/default.asp (Accessed April 30, 2022).
3. Rajya Sabha, 'Defence deals between India and Israel', Unstarred Question 4481, May 16, 2007, at https://rajyasabha.nic.in/rsnew/Questions/QResult.aspx (Accessed August 20, 2021).
4. Rajya Sabha, 'Establishing chemical plants in Bihar by Israel', Unstarred Question 1786, August 10, 2005, at https://rajyasabha.nic.in/rsnew/Questions/QResult.aspx (Accessed August 20, 2021).
5. Pieter D. Wezeman, Alexandra Kuimova and Siemon T. Wezeman, 'Trends in international arms transfers 2020', Stockholm International Peace Research Institute, March 2021, p. 2, at https://sipri.org/sites/default/files/2021-03/fs_2103_at_2020.pdf (Accessed August 25, 2021).
6. Pieter D. Wezeman, Alexandra Kuimova and Siemon T. Wezeman, 'Trends in international arms transfers 2021', Stockholm International Peace Research Institute, March 2022, p. 2, at https://www.sipri.org/sites/default/files/2022-03/fs_2203_at_2021.pdf (Accessed May 5, 2022).
7. SIPRI, 'TIV of arms exports from Israel, 2000-2021' at https://armstrade.sipri.org/armstrade/page/values.php (Accessed May 5, 2022).
8. Pieter D. Wezeman, et. al, no. 6, p. 6.
9. Ibid., p. 9.
10. Pieter D. Wezeman, et. al, no. 5, p. 6.
11. Ibid., p. 2.
12. Pieter D. Wezeman, et. al, no. 6, p. 2.
13. Harsh V. Pant, 'A Fine Balance: India Walks a Tightrope between Iran and the United States', *Orbis*, Summer 2007; Sushil J. Aaron, 'Straddling Faultlines: India's Foreign Policy towards the Greater Middle East', CSH Occasional Paper No. 7, August 2003, at http://www.csh-delhi.com/publications/downloads/ops/OP7.pdf (Accessed April 25, 2011); S. Samuel C. Rajiv, 'The Delicate Balance: Israel and India's Foreign Policy Practice', *Strategic Analysis*, 36 (1), January 2012, pp. 128-144; See also Elliot Jager, 'Limited Partnership', August 16, 2010 at

http://www.jewishideasdaily.com/content/module/2010/8/16/main-feature/1/limited-partnership (Accessed April 25, 2011).

14. Ministry of External Affairs, 'Delhi Statement on Friendship and Cooperation between India and Israel', September 10, 2003 at https://mea.gov.in/bilateral-documents.htm?dtl/7730/Delhi+Statement+on+Friendship+and+Cooperation+between+India+and+Israel (Accessed August 25, 2021).
15. Ministry of External Affairs, 'Transcript of Media Briefing by External Affairs Minister on Completing One Year in Government', May 31, 2015 at https://www.mea.gov.in/media-briefings.htm?dtl/25304/Transcript+of+Media+Briefing+by+External+Affairs+ Minister+ on+ Completing+One+Year+in+Government+May+31+2015 (Accessed September 10, 2021).
16. Rajya Sabha, "Rulings by the Chair", July 17, 2014, p. 1 at http://rsdebate.nic.in/bitstream/123456789/631895/2/PD_232_17072014_p1_p12_2.pdf#search=gaza (Accessed September 10, 2021).
17. For an analysis of the parliamentary debate, see S. Samuel C. Rajiv, *Indian Responses to Israel's Gaza Operations*, Mideast Security and Policy Studies No. 119, BESA Center for Strategic Studies, May 2016, pp. 37-48.
18. Amit Baruah, 'India may end support to Palestine at UN', *The Hindu*, December 21, 2014, at http://www.thehindu.com/news/national/india-may-end-support-to-palestine-at-un/article6713364.ece (Accessed September 20, 2021).
19. Ministry of External Affairs, 'India-Israel Joint Statement during the visit of Prime Minister to Israel', July 5, 2017, at https://www.mea.gov.in/bilateral-documents.htm?dtl/28593/IndiaIsrael_Joint_Statement_during_the_visit_of_Prime_Minister_to_Israel_July_5_2017 (Accessed July 6, 2017).
20. Caroline B. Glick, 'Modi and Israel's coming of age', *Jerusalem Post*, July 3, 2017, at http://www.jpost.com/Opinion/Our-World-Modi-and-Israels-coming-of-age-498671 (Accessed July 4, 2017); P.R. Kumaraswamy, 'Modi in Israel: PM has done the groundwork, will business giants follow suit?', July 7, 2017, at http://www.hindustantimes.com/opinion/modi-in-israel-pm-has-done-the-groundwork-will-business-giants-follow-suit/story-446EPyhQRz5oSqNSFbZH8L.htm (Accessed September 20, 2021); P.R. Kumaraswamy, 'Modi redefines India's Palestine Policy', IDSA Issue Brief, May 18, 2017, at https://www.idsa.in/issuebrief/modi-redefines-india-palestine-policy_prkumaraswamy_180517 (Accessed September 20, 2017).
21. Ministry of External Affairs, 'India-Israel Joint Statement during visit of Prime Minister of Israel to India', January 15, 2018, at https://www.mea.gov.in/bilateral-documents.htm?dtl/29357/IndiaIsrael+Joint+Statement+during+visit+of+Prime+Minister+of+Israel+to+ India+January+15+2018 (Accessed January 16, 2018);
22. Ministry of External Affairs, 'Remarks of External Affairs Minister after meeting with APM and FM Yair Lapid of Israel', October 18, 2021, at https://www.mea.gov.in/Speeches-Statements.htm?dtl/34400/Remarks+of+External+Affairs+Minister+after+meeting+with+APM+ and+ FM+ Yair+ Lapid+ of+ Israel+October+18+2021 (Accessed October 19, 2021).

2

DEFENCE COOPERATION

India-Israel defence and security cooperation has witnessed tremendous growth, after full diplomatic ties were established in January 1992. Even during the period when full diplomatic relations were not established, India sought Israeli security assistance. This was most prominent during the 1965 and 1971 India-Pakistan conflicts. The equipment supplied by Israel for these wars, like 160 mm mortars, also saw action two decades later, during the 1999 Kargil War.[1] Post-1992, defence and security cooperation have constituted the key pillar of the India-Israel strategic partnership. India has procured cutting-edge equipment from Israel to plug critical security needs and help in the modernization of its armed forces. The inability of the Indian defence industry to cater to these requirements also necessitated that India seek such equipment from overseas.

Israel, on its part, exhibited political will to provide niche equipment to India, unencumbered by restrictions on such transfers by Israel's close ally, the United States (US). The US, for instance, prevented Israel from going ahead with the 1998 contract with China for airborne early warning and control aircraft (AWACS). Due to US pressure, the contract was terminated in 2000, with Israel even having to pay damages for not fulfilling the terms of the contract. The US put pressure on Israel over fears that such niche capabilities could aid Beijing's efforts to forcefully take over Taiwan.

During Prime Minister Narendra Modi's July 2017 visit to Israel—the first Indian prime ministerial visit in 25 years, both countries formally acknowledged their 'strategic partnership'. This chapter places the defence aspects of the India-Israel strategic partnership in historical and contemporary perspective.

Contours of Cooperation

After the establishment of diplomatic ties in 1992, India has gradually increased the volume of defence purchases from Israel, beginning in 1996-1997 with the procurement of the Searcher unmanned aerial vehicles (UAVs) – with the initial contract dating back to 1996, and Super Dvora patrol boats. India's defence ties with Israel were strengthened in the aftermath of the Kargil conflict. India secured key equipment like ammunition for its artillery guns. India has since procured a wide range of equipment, from assault rifles to the Phalcon airborne warning and control systems (AWACS), fire-control radars, missiles, among a host of other equipment.[2] The following sections delineate key aspects of the bilateral defence cooperation, primarily focusing on procurement and joint development programmes related to three broad areas – surveillance capabilities; missiles; and niche equipment encompassing assault weapons to aircraft parts.

Surveillance Platforms and Equipment

India has procured key equipment like UAVs, AWACS and radars to plug deficiencies in the surveillance capabilities of its armed forces. India has used the Israeli-made UAVs for significantly enhancing its security operations along its coastline as well as for internal security purposes. India procured more than 150 Searcher and Heron UAVs, made by Israel Aerospace Industries (IAI). The latter is a medium-altitude long-endurance (MALE) UAV—capable of flying non-stop for more than 50 hours, while the former can fly up to 18 hours. The Western Naval Command commissioned its first UAV squadron made up of Israeli-procured UAVs in January 2011 at Porbandar, Gujarat, five years after the first UAV squadron was commissioned at Kochi.[3]

The then Chief of Naval Staff, Admiral Arun Prakash, inaugurating the Kochi squadron, stated that the Israeli UAVs were being inducted after three years of flying trials and that the Indian Navy was 'now amongst the pioneers in the esoteric art of UAV operation at sea'.[4] Admiral Prakash emphasized that the Israeli assets would enhance the country's 'maritime domain awareness manifold'. A third UAV squadron made up of Searchers and Herons was set up along the Tamil Nadu coast in 2012.[5] In 2019, India reportedly signed a $500 million contract with the IAI for 50 additional Heron UAVs.[6]

Apart from the Herons and the Searchers, the IAI also has in its stable, the Heron-Turbo Prop (TP) unmanned combat aerial system (UAS). It is described as an advanced multi-role, long range, MALE UAV for 'strategic missions', equipped with satellite communication systems, automatic take-off and landing, an endurance of more than 30 hours and capable of carrying a variety of lethal and surveillance payloads.[7] As against the Heron, which has a payload weight of about 500 kg, the Heron-TP is advertised to carry multiple payloads five times that weight. The maximum payload weight of the Searcher tactical UAV, meanwhile, is about 100 kg. The Israeli Air Force is the only Air Force currently operating the Heron-TP system.

Reports in mid-2018 noted that India had decided to procure at least ten Heron-TP drones, at a cost of $400 million, to enhance the country's 'cross-border military strike' capability.[8] Pertinently, this alluded to possible usage of the drone across India's western front. Reports in 2021, however, noted that India will lease four Heron-TPs for use in the eastern sector, given the changed security situation along the China border. The leased Heron-TPs are reportedly non-lethal, to be used solely for surveillance purposes.[9] By December 2021, these drones have reportedly been deployed on the border.[10]

The leasing of the Heron-TPs was the second such procurement decision to make use of the leasing provisions of the Defence Acquisition Procedure 2020. Two General Atomic MQ-9B Sea Guardian drones have been leased by the Indian Navy. The IAI on its part is a veteran in leasing arrangements, with its drones leased to countries like Canada, Australia and Spain.[11]

India will have one of the few armed forces in the world to use the Heron-TP, apart from Israel. Reports in August 2021 also noted that the Indian armed forces will undertake a massive modernization exercise involving the Israeli UAV's in its arsenal, amounting to over Rs 5000 crores. The programme seeks to even arm previously-procured Herons as well as improve their surveillance capabilities.[12]

Hindustan Aeronautics Limited (HAL), along with Dynamatic Technologies Limited (DTL), signed a strategic partnership agreement with the IAI at the Defence Expo 2020, for marketing, manufacture and sale of UAVs.[13] HAL also signed an MoU with Elbit Systems for exploring the feasibility of joint development and production of 2000 kg vertical take-off and landing (VTOL) UAVs for both maritime and land-based operations for domestic as well as international customers.

The March 2004 deal with Elta for three Phalcon AWACS worth $1.1 billion, has been one of the largest defence deals that India has concluded with Israel. The first and second AWACS aircraft were delivered in May 2009 and March 2010, while the third was delivered in mid-2011. The Rajya Sabha had been informed in May 2010 that procurement of additional AWACS aircraft was on the anvil.[14]

India, though, is increasingly focusing on indigenous procurement of such assets. India has two indigenous airborne early warning and control (AEW&C) systems mounted on Embraer aircraft—*Netra*, in its inventory.[15] The first of the aircraft was handed to the IAF in February 2017.[16] The *Netra* aircraft took part in the Balakot surgical strikes in February 2019.[17]

Meanwhile, reports in December 2020 noted that India intends to spend more than Rs 10,000 crores to equip its Air Force with six additional AWACS aircraft. The DRDO would acquire six Airbus aircraft from the Air India fleet (319/320/321), and equip them with indigenously developed active electronically scanned array (AESA) radars.[18] The original Request for Proposal (RfP) for six AWACS was issued in 2014 but uncertainty over choice of the aircraft to mount the radar, among other issues, delayed the decision.[19] In September 2021, the Cabinet Committee on Security (CCS) finally approved the Acceptance of Necessity (AoN) for the DRDO to issue the Request for Proposal (RfP) to procure the aircraft.[20]

Apart from UAVs and AWACS, India has bought a whole range of radars from Israel for its aircrafts, ships and land forces. One of the earliest radars that India bought was the ground surveillance/battlefield surveillance radar

(BFSR) EL/M-2140 in 1998, with the ability to detect tanks/vehicles/troops up to a range of 40 km.[21] The range of the Israeli radars was subsequently expanded to enable beyond line-of-sight (LOS) detection.[22] A large number of Elta's air search radars for use on frontline warships like frigates, destroyers and aircraft carriers have been procured. The EL/M-2221 fire control radar was bought for use along with the Barak-I surface-to-air missile (SAM) system, a point defence system installed on many warships.

Combat aircraft radars for purposes of modernization of aircraft like the Jaguars began to be procured from 1999 onwards. While the initial combat radars were 'mechanically steered array' (MSA) radars, Elta subsequently provided AESA radars (with the first Jaguar fitted with the radar flying in 2018), making the Jaguar the first combat aircraft in India's inventory to be fitted with these advanced radars.[23]

Multi-mode radars, co-developed with Elta, have been integrated into the Light Combat Aircraft (LCA).[24] The EL/M-2052 AESA radars replaced Elta's manual EL/M-2032 radars in the LCA, as indeed in aircrafts such as Jaguar (in 2018 as noted above) and on Mirages in India's inventory.[25] The LCA's Helmet-Mounted Display and Sight (HMDS) is also provided by the Israeli company, Elbit.

The contract with Rafael Advanced Defence Systems for two aerostat radars was entered into in 2002, at a cost of around Rs 676 crores ($145 million), to meet the requirements of low-level surveillance. The radars, positioned at a height of around 14,000 feet, can detect low-flying aircraft at a distance of 250 km. These were commissioned in 2007 and 2008, respectively.[26]

The country's first indigenous aerostat radar, *Akashdeep,* launched in 2010, was developed by the Aerial Delivery Research Development Establishment (ADRDE). The maiden flight of an improved version, *Nakshatra,* was conducted in October 2015 about 22 months after the project began in January 2014.[27] However, within a year, the project was closed due to difficulties with the indigenously-designed laminated fabric material that made up the balloon housing the radar.[28] ADRDE officials however insisted that the Army did not provide funds to carry out additional user trials and therefore, the project was shelved.[29] Reports in February 2016 noted that the IAF was looking to acquire at least six aerostat radars to meet its operational requirements.[30]

Missiles

The Rs 2,600 crore contract for the joint development of long-range surface-to-air missile (LRSAM) for the Indian Navy (IN) was signed in January 2006. The system, with a range of 70 km, is used for ensuring point and area defence against a variety of threats, including aircrafts and missiles. The DRDO handed over the first batch of five LRSAM missiles to the Indian Navy in 2017.[31] The initial test firing of the missile was conducted off the coast of Chennai in December 2015.[32] In January 2019, *INS Chennai* and *INS Kolkata* successfully conducted the Joint Target Coordination (JTC) firing of the LRSAM system.[33] The final production batch was handed over to the IN in February 2021. The missile's indigenous content includes its dual-pulse rocket motor.[34] The IAI provides the Multi-Function Surveillance and Threat Alert Radar (MF-STAR).

The Rs 10,000 crores contract for the joint development of medium-range SAM (MRSAM) for the IAF was concluded in 2009. India and Israel signed a MoU worth $1.6 billion for MRSAMs for use by the Indian Army in April 2017. The first test of the system was done in December 2020.[35] The Indo-Israel joint venture, Kalyani Rafael Advanced Systems (KRAS), produces MRSAM missile kits for integration by the public sector Bharat Dynamics Limited (BDL). The IAF has also procured the Spyder low-level quick reaction surface-to-air missile (LLQRM) systems equipped with Python and Derby missiles for protection against aerial targets, including aircraft, cruise missiles and UAVs.

The contract for the procurement of Barak-1 missiles for Indian Navy warships was signed in October 2014 with Rafael Advanced Defence Systems Ltd., at a cost of Rs 875.49 crores.[36] The Barak protects a wide range of ships, including destroyers and frigates. In September 2013, reports flagged shortages of missiles and the efforts to replenish them were facing difficulties, because of an anti-corruption probe by the Central Bureau of Investigation (CBI) against individuals who had allegedly received kickbacks for the October 2000 deal. The IAI was placed on the MoD blacklist in 2006, because of the CBI investigation. This impacted the procurement of missiles for the warships. Due to 'paucity of evidence', the CBI closed the case, paving the way for the Indian Navy to buy the missiles from IAI. By December 2013, India placed an order for nearly Rs. 880 crores ($150 million) to buy 262 missiles.[37] While a special court accepted the closure report of the CBI in January 2017, it was not until April 2018, however, that Rafael was taken off the MoD's blacklist.[38]

The orders for Spike anti-tank guided missiles (ATGMs) are a unique example of the dynamics associated with the India-Israel defence partnership. The December 2020 orders—as well as orders for more than 200 Spike missiles in the aftermath of the Balakot strikes in February 2019, signified operational imperatives guiding procurement decisions, amidst lack of viable, domestic alternatives.

These orders came despite the Government announcing in late 2017—just ahead of Prime Minister Netanyahu's visit in January 2018—that it was not proceeding with importing the systems for the Indian armed forces, ostensibly in favour of inducting indigenous systems like the *Nag*.[39] Reports in January 2018 flagged that the Army had an ominous shortage of ATGMs in its inventory—to the tune of nearly 70,000 ATGMs.[40] When this report was brought to the attention of the Government in the Lok Sabha, Minister of State for Defence, Subhash Bhamre affirmed that the Government was taking appropriate measures to maintain 'desire(d) level of operational preparedness commensurate to the threat perception in a dynamic strategic scenario'.[41]

In October 2014, India's Defence Acquisition Council (DAC), headed by the Defence Minister, gave the go-ahead for procuring 8,000 Spike ATGM, valued at over $500 million. The Acceptance of Necessity (AoN) for the missiles was given earlier in June 2009 for procuring 8356 missiles and 321 launchers under 'Buy and Make' category of the Defence Procurement Procedure with transfer of technology (ToT) to Bharat Dynamics Limited (BDL). The Spike missile was preferred over other competitors like the US-made Javelin ATGM. The Javelin offer by the US was a component of the Defence Trade and Technology Initiative (DTTI) for co-development and manufacture.[42] The Request for Proposal (RfP) for the missiles was issued in April 2010.

The Spike saga unfolded in the backdrop of the huge requirement for third-generation ATGMs in the Indian armed forces, which had in its inventory second-generation ATGMs like the 'wire-guided' Russian-made Konkurs-M and the French Milan systems. The Government's auditor, the CAG, in 2010, also expressed concern over the Army continuing with its procurement of second- generation ATGMs like Milan, despite the availability of third-generation ATGMs globally.[43]

Delays in development of indigenous ATGMs like the *Nag*, further added to the woes of the armed forces. The testing of the missile began as far back as the 1990s. In user trials specifically in desert conditions, problems with the missile's imaging infra-red (IIR) seeker guidance system were detected.[44] After modifications, orders for over 400 missiles were placed by the Army in 2010.

Even as reports in 2015 indicated that the Spike deal was facing delays due to issues over price negotiations, India did go ahead with finalizing the contract and the stage was set for inducting the Israeli systems.[45] The Spike RfP, issued in 2010, was, however, retracted on December 20, 2017. Defence Minister Nirmala Sitharaman informed Parliament that the decision was taken to encourage 'indigenous' development of the ATGM by the DRDO.[46]

With reports noting that the Nag missile was ready for induction—the final user trials were conducted in October 2020, cutting-edge and cheaper technologies for use in man-portable ATGMs are being developed by indigenous start-ups like Tonbo Imaging Private Limited. While systems like the Nag (and the Spike) use costlier, cooled IIR seekers, Tonbo developed uncooled IIR seekers, which were also lightweight and better suited for man-portable ATGMs.[47]

Assault Weapons, Ammunition, Niche Aircraft Parts

Apart from the significant cooperation relating to UAVs, AWACS, radars and missiles, India and Israel have cooperated in the field of assault weapons, ammunition, niche aircraft parts, among other critical equipment. The HAL has longstanding cooperation with Israeli firms and their subsidiaries like the IAI and Elbit Systems. HAL's Korwa plant, entered into a MoU with Elbit subsidiary Elop Electro-Optics Industries Limited in 2003 to manufacture Head-Up Displays (HUD) for IAF aircraft. Over 500 such displays have been integrated into various IAF platforms like Su-30MKI, Jaguar and MiG-27M.[48]

At the Aero India 2021, HAL entered into an agreement for digital overhead HUDs (used widely in transport aircraft) with the same company. IAI and HAL also have an agreement for the supply of main deck cargo doors for Boeing 737 aircraft. In joint development programmes, electronic warfare

(EW) suites have been co-developed in association with Elisra, for the Light Combat Aircraft (LCA), *Tejas*. Elisra was also involved in co-developing the Dual Colour Missile Approach Warning System (DCMAWS) for the Su-30 MKI aircraft.

Artillery ammunition was developed by three ordnance factories (Ambajhari, Kanpur, and Chandrapur) in association with Israel Weapons Industries (IWI).[49] For India's Special Forces, 5.56 mm Tavor assault rifles, were bought in 2005 at a cost of $18 million.[50] Israeli Smart, Precise Impact, Cost-Effective (SPICE) guided ammunition kits were used in the February 2019 Balakot air strikes by the Indian Air Force (IAF) inside Pakistan-occupied Kashmir (PoK). Reports in December 2020 noted that India ordered additional SPICE kits for $200 million, along with Spike ATGMs.[51]

The Indian Army also uses the Negev NG-7 light machine gun (LMG); an order over 16,000 such guns was placed in 2020 to combat the increasing ceasefire violations by Pakistan at the Line of Control. In November 2021, SSS Defence—a division of the manufacturing firm, Stumpp, Schuele and Somappa Springs Private Limited Ltd, edged out an Israeli firm to upgrade limited numbers of AK-47 rifles of the Jaipur-based Southwestern Command.[52] SSS Defence, in fact, is only the second private sector small arms manufacturer to win orders from the MoD, after PLR Systems, in which, incidentally, the Israel Weapons Industries (IWI) has a stake.[53]

Institutional Interactions and Military Exercises

Robust interactions among the defence forces is an essential component of the India-Israel strategic interaction. The India-Israel Joint Committee on Defence Cooperation met for the first time in September 2002. As part of defence diplomacy, while there has been a constant stream of visits of Indian Naval ships to Haifa, as many as ten heads of defence forces from each side have visited the other country in the past 25 years (See Appendix).

Joint working groups (JWGs) on defence cooperation, helmed by the respective MoDs, as well as consultations by the Foreign Ministries, are an essential feature of such institutionalized cooperation. The 16th round of Foreign Office Consultations, for instance, were held in December 2020, in virtual mode, where the entire gamut of the bilateral relations were reviewed, including issues relating to defence and security, water, counter-terrorism, cyber security, science and technology and innovation cooperation.[54] At the 15th India-Israel Joint Working Group (JWG) on defence, held in Tel Aviv in October 2021, both countries agreed to set up a sub-working group (SWG) on defence industry cooperation.[55] A SWG on Defence Procurement, Development and Production is functional.

Indian and Israeli forces also take part in joint exercises to learn from each other's best practices. The Blue Flag Exercises conducted by the Israeli Air Force (IsAF) are an important facet of Israel's military diplomacy. The first Blue Flag Exercises took place in November 2013 and since then the multilateral Exercises have acquired a quiet momentum. A 45-member Indian Air Force (IAF) contingent, including *Garud* commandos, along with a C-130J special operations aircraft, participated in these exercises for the first time in 2017. France, Germany, Greece, Italy, Poland and the United States were the other participating countries in the 2017 event.

While participation by other nations involved fighter aircraft at this event, India sent the special operations transport aircraft. Given the presence of *Garud* commandos, the C-130J was a tactical choice in order to enable them to be exposed to best counter-terrorism practices from the Israeli experience. Another factor that could have precluded participation of a fighter aircraft was the need for over-flight clearance from countries in the Gulf which do not have diplomatic relations with Israel. This factor, in the aftermath of the Abraham Accords of September 2020, has, however, significantly diminished. The Indian C-130J, meanwhile, reportedly had a stop-over in Egypt, on its journey to the Uvda Air Force Base, the base conducting the Blue Flag Exercises. Even prior to India's first ever participation in the Blue Flag Exercises, commentators had opined that the presence of American aircraft like the C-130J in India's inventory creates 'a certain degree of commonality with IsAF platforms.'[56]

India's participation in the 2021 iteration of the Blue Flag Exercises saw the involvement of IAF's Mirage 2000 as well as Rafale aircraft. External Affairs Minster S. Jaishankar, who was also visiting Israel during that time, interacted with the fighter pilots participating in these exercises from other countries. After the event in Israel, the IAF contingent also participated in air exercises in Egypt. In March 2021, the IAF had also participated in air exercises in the

United Arab Emirates (UAE) for the first time. The UAE exercises saw the participation of the US, French, Saudi Arabian, South Korean, and Bahraini air forces.

Joint military exercises play an important role in military forces getting familiar with the operating procedures and best practices of each country. While India does not conduct multilateral air exercises on its soil, it is a part of significant numbers of military exercises involving the armies, navies and air forces across the world. For Israel, the United States and countries in Europe continue to be the main training partners.

Commentators have also flagged the promise of naval exercises between India and Israel, given the mutual complementarities and interests of both countries in the waters of the Indian Ocean and the Mediterranean Sea. The Israeli Navy is a potent regional force. Israel, though a 'brown water' navy, is still equipped with significant naval capabilities in the form of the German-sourced Dolphin submarines as well as Saar-5 corvettes. Reports have also flagged that Israel has been testing long- range missiles in the waters of the Indian Ocean.

India and Israel, meanwhile, have had long-standing relationship in the naval field. Apart from military diplomacy in the form of visits of Indian naval ships at the Haifa port, India secured Israeli patrol boats (Super Dvora Mk-11) in the 1990s. Niche Israeli equipment is an essential part of frontline Indian naval warships, including radars and point defence missiles like the Barak, as flagged in previous sections.

Analysts note that Israel's interests increasingly encompass the waters of the Indian Ocean, apart from the country's core interests in the waters surrounding it, like the Mediterranean Sea and the Red Sea. This is due to its on-going geo-political rivalry with countries like Iran. India-Israel interests also converge on issues such as maritime terrorism, concerns over proliferation of weapons of mass destruction, among others. India could also be a significant partner of the Israeli Navy in offering logistical support to its deployed vessels. India and Israel, going forward, could also explore opportunities for greater engagement relating to 'non-contentious' areas like humanitarian assistance and disaster relief and protection of sea lanes of communication.[57]

Enablers for Defence Cooperation

India's procurement of niche defence equipment from Israel was necessitated by the need to more effectively address the growing regional, cross-border as well as internal security challenges. India's external security environment has become more challenging in the past decades, on account of the terrorist threat emanating from Pakistan's safe havens, the collusion between Pakistan and China in the strategic domain—including nuclear, missile and defence technology cooperation—and China's increasingly belligerent actions on the Line of Actual Control (LAC) as well as on India's periphery. Defence Minister George Fernandes, for instance, in as early as 1998, had flagged Chinese construction of electronic surveillance equipment on the Coco Islands since 1994.[58]

The 1999 Kargil conflict highlighted gaps in surveillance and intelligence capabilities of the armed forces. The 26/11 terror strikes in Mumbai highlighted gaps in coastal surveillance. Even successful cross-border strikes as in Balakot in February 2019, as well as India's recent border tensions with China, revealed the need for multiple systems for greater effectiveness.[59] The modernization requirements of India's armed forces, meanwhile, continue to be gargantuan. Israel's niche technological prowess, in supplying key equipment like avionics, radars, missiles, point defence systems, among others, has gelled well with the country's requirements of these niche equipment.

The failure of developmental efforts of indigenous weapons systems has led India to procure similar equipment from Israel. India's indigenous efforts to develop an aerial surveillance platform (ASP), for instance, suffered a setback, when an Avro HS-748 test aircraft, crashed in January 1999. The DRDO had initiated the ASP programme in 1985, at a cost of Rs 52.09 crores. After the crash, Defence Minister Jaswant Singh informed Parliament that the programme was 'short-closed'.[60]

Defence Minister George Fernandes in April 2000 admitted that delays in indigenous development of critical technologies as well as sanctions imposed after India conducted the nuclear tests in 1998 had negatively impacted a wide range of programmes. These included the light combat aircraft (LCA), remotely piloted vehicle (RPV) *Nishant*, anti-tank missile system, *Nag* and the integrated electronic warfare (EW) system for the Army.[61]

Fernandes informed the Rajya Sabha in August 2000 that 'technological problems associated with indigenous developments' were responsible for the delay in the development of *Nishant* pilotless aircraft.[62] The procurement of the Israeli Barak point defence system was an essential requirement to protect frontline assets of the Indian Navy, given that the indigenous Trishul system failed in user trials. Defence Minister Manohar Parrikar, while touting the indigenous achievements of the DRDO, in response to a query in Parliament in 2016, did note that the import content of the indigenously developed AEW&C system (excluding the Embraer aircraft) was still pegged at 16 per cent.[63]

The CAG in 2018 pointed out that there was 'inordinate delay' in the indigenous development of UAVs by the DRDO. Those that were developed 'failed to meet the requirements of the Indian Army'. The CAG also pointed out that delays in development of MALE UAVs 'adversely affected the aerial surveillance capabilities of the Indian Army'.[64] The MALE UAV project was sanctioned in February 2011 with a total cost of over Rs 1500 crores but the 2018 CAG report noted that there were 'multiple issues' with the development project, including with the airframe, line replaceable units (LRU), engine and payload.[65] Reports highlighting the conclusion of a strategic partnership agreement between the IAI, HAL and Dynamatic Technologies Limited (DTL) in February 2020 pointed out that the Rustom-II MALE UAV being indigenously developed by the DRDO crashed during flight trials in September 2019.[66]

As with the UAVs, India had to procure Israeli radars due to non-availability of similar domestically developed products for optimum surveillance coverage on its Western borders. The DRDO lab, the Aerial Delivery Research Development Establishment (ADRDE), first tested an indigenous aerostat radar (*Aakashdeep*) in December 2010. Audit reports have also highlighted delays in execution of projects due to inconsistencies in monitoring of the projects, change of requirements by the user (the armed forces) and lack of cohesion among multiple agencies executing the projects. The CAG Report No. 38 in 2015, for instance, highlighted the closure of several radar projects like *Rohini*, *Aslesha*, and *Revathy* by the DRDO.[67]

Even as successive Israeli governments have nurtured strategic ties with

India assiduously, their transfer was not vetoed by the United States, which was involved in developing some of the niche equipment that India procured from Israel. The US, for instance, vetoed the sale of the Phalcon AWACS to China. Israel went back on the 1998 contract to supply AWACS to Beijing in July 2000, on account of American pressure and had to even pay a penalty for its decision.

The US, though, vetoed the sale of sophisticated missile defence systems like the Arrow to India. India's request for Arrow followed its open embrace of President George W. Bush's missile defence plans. The Bush administration championed missile defence as an effective deterrent to face the threats posed by the 'rogue' states like Iran, Iraq and Libya, especially so in the aftermath of the September 2001 terror strikes in New York.

The US Department of State in July 2002 acknowledged that there was an Israeli request for transferring the Arrow system to India but that it gives importance to strategic stability in South Asia and to the Missile Technology Control Regime (MTCR).[68] Analysts noted that India evaluating the Arrow was in the context of plugging gaps in its air defence architecture, and that it preferred the system over comparative systems from Russia like the S-300.[69] India did become a member of the MTCR in June 2016 and has since procured an even more advanced version, the S-400, from the Russian Federation.

This deal continues to be under the sanctions cloud of the US, following the passage of the Comprehensive American Sanctions and Divestment Act (CAATSA) in July 2017, on account of Russia's actions in Ukraine, among other places. Apart from India, Turkiye's decision to go in for the S-400 system, has invited an American backlash. Ankara had to suffer consequences, including being shut out of the F-35 programme, in which it had a significant part.

Interactions between the foreign policy and national security establishments of both India and the US, meanwhile, are a continuing process to overcome the disadvantages posed by CAATSA. This, even as India-US defence trade has grown by leaps and bounds in recent times. The extent to which US sanctions targeting Russia for its February 2022 invasion of Ukraine would affect India-Russia defence trade, remains to be seen. Reports say that US sanctions could hit deliveries of the S-400 as well as other key procurement programmes like *Talwar*-class frigates (which are equipped with engines made in Ukraine).[70]

Israel was able to address India's growing defence requirements given its capabilities in such niche technology areas like UAVs and surveillance systems. Elta's AESA radar used in the Phalcon system, for instance, was touted as superior to that of mechanically rotating antennas, then used widely, endowing the system with 'greater operational flexibility....'[71]

The prowess of the Israeli systems was in contrast to the capabilities of other comparable systems that India tested in trials. Defence Minister George Fernandes informed the Upper House of Parliament in August 2000 that 'the performance of the Russian A-50 AWACS, as observed during the demonstrations, did not meet the requirements of Indian Air Force'.[72] The Defence Minister's comments were after the A-50 was taken on lease for a period of 30 days to test its effectiveness and suitability.[73]

Israeli companies have also been successful in bidding for contracts, given India's procurement policy framework, which privileges awarding the contract to the lowest bidder. The relative price advantage ostensibly helps them win the contract, which favours the lowest bidder. Elta, for instance, in 2007, was the lowest bidder in response to a request for proposals (RfP) for medium-power radars for the Indian Air Force in a contract worth over Rs 800 crores. It is equally true that India did not go ahead with critical procurements like additional Phalcon AWACS when Israel and Russia quoted higher prices.[74]

More recently, the Israeli firm, Elbit, quoted a cheaper price than a French gun-maker in a government tender to supply towed artillery guns. Further, the firm also offered to make 70 per cent of the order in India, which was more than 50 per cent of the requirement, and offered to provide faster transfer of technology.[75] Reports, though, noted that the MoD did not finally go ahead with the Israeli offer for artillery guns, and instead focused on the DRDO-designed Advanced Towed Artillery Gun System (ATAGS), as well as procurement of the Larsen and Toubro-made K9 *Vajra* guns, made in collaboration with a South Korean defence firm, to fill operational gaps in the Eastern sector.[76]

Israeli defence companies, meanwhile, invest substantially in research and development (R&D) to maintain their lead in terms of innovation. The IAI, for instance, lays a premium on innovation and is a corporate partner in domestic as well as global start-up accelerators like Starburst. Its US unit is part of the New Space Consortium, consisting of Lockheed Martin, US Air Force, NASA, MAXAR and SAIC. Seventy-five per cent of IAI's sales ($3 billion in 2019; $4.2 billion in 2020; $4.5 billion in 2021) are to export markets. The company's sales in 2021 were the highest in its history. The IAI spent over $1 billion on R&D in 2021, more than the $900 million it had spent in 2019. The company's profits in 2021 were $696 million, an increase on over 15 per cent from the previous year.[77] The IAI is one of Israel's largest industrial exporters and employers, with 16,000 employees.

The IAI's main domestic competitor, Rafael Advanced Defence Systems Limited, had sales of over $3 billion (as against $2.8 billion in 2020) and an order backlog of over $7 billion. The company makes the Iron Dome point defence system, as well as the Spike and SPICE bombs, among a plethora of cutting-edge equipment. The company invests close to 10 per cent of its sales on R&D.[78]

Israel has continued to maintain its position as one of the biggest arms exporters in the world. During 2016-20, Israel was the eighth-largest arms exporter in the world, behind the US, Russia, France, Germany, China, the United Kingdom and Spain. Cutting-edge, niche equipment like missiles and sensors overwhelmingly make up the quantum of defence exports from Israel.

Israel is also one of the world's largest exporters of UAVs. During 2005-2012, one study noted that Israel exported $4.6 billion worth of UAVs. At least half of these exports were to countries in Europe, like the United Kingdom, which procured a large number of Israeli Hermes 450 UAVs.[79] By 2017, it was estimated that Israel supplied close to 60 per cent of global UAV exports. At least 50 countries operate Israeli-made UAVs.[80] Out of the total Israeli military exports in 2020 estimated at $8 billion, the exports of UAVs accounted for at least $500 million, or six per cent of total sales, as per reports.[81] In October 2021, the Israel Air Force marked the 50th anniversary of operational use of UAVs. Such long-standing use, robust R&D investments, with an emphasis on innovation-led growth, will, no doubt, continue to enhance the value of the Israeli defence industrial base and help promote defence exports as well.

Critics of the Defence Relationship

A common feature across different governments is the stress on non-disclosure as regards India-Israel defence cooperation. Defence Minister Fernandes, in November 2001, when asked in the Rajya Sabha if India had signed defence deals with Israel amounting to $2 billion, stated that while India was signing defence contracts with Israel, it was 'not in the interest of national security' to give details as to the nature of those contracts.[82]

Defence Minister Antony told the Lok Sabha in November 2007 that:

> Procurement/acquisition of items to meet defence requirements of the armed forces is made from various indigenous as well as foreign sources including Israel. ... Divulging details in this regard would not be in the interest of national security.[83]

Responding to a query from Sitaram Yechury of the CPI (M) on the purchase of missiles from Israel, Antony insisted that 'divulging details ... would not be in the interest of national security'.[84] Anthony, again, six years later in 2013, repeated the same national security argument when the government was asked by Chandan Mitra if India and Israel were jointly developing anti-missile defence systems.[85]

Anthony's successor, Manohar Parrikar, in December 2014, when asked whether the Government had signed a new defence equipment purchase with Israel, stated that while two capital procurement contracts were signed with Israeli vendors during the financial year, 'divulging of details will not be in the interest of national security'.[86] As noted earlier, the Government only on two occasions—in August 2005 and May 2007—disclosed data relating to the estimated financial volume of the India-Israel defence relationship.

Successive government's policy positions on not divulging details about the nature and quantum of the India-Israel defence trade, is, no doubt, justified on account of national security considerations. There is, however, a better appreciation of the financial volume of India's other critical defence relationships, like the India-US defence relationship. The opacity surrounding the India-Israel defence relationship, specifically on aspects relating to financial volume, therefore, leaves space for critics to raise issues about the nature of the relationship.

After the Indian government cancelled the Spike ATGM deal in 2017, just ahead of Prime Minister Netanyahu's visit to India in January 2018, critics of India's defence engagement with Israel stated that the decision was a 'huge blow' to the Israeli weapons industry.[87] Such critics, though, discount the fact that the Spike ATGM is currently in the inventory of the armed forces of more than 30 countries. India, has also subsequently re-entered into contracts with the Israeli defence company, Rafael, for the supply of the Spike ATGM, to fulfil critical operational requirements.

During the discussion in the Indian Parliament on Israel's 2014 military operation in the Gaza Strip—Protective Edge—when the opposition demanded the passing of a Resolution critical of Israel, some lawmakers demanded that India stop its military cooperation with Israel. The Member of Parliament from Hyderabad, Asaduddin Owaisi, as well as CPI(M)'s Sitaram Yechury called for an end to the defence relationship with Israel.[88] Foreign Minister Sushma Swaraj, however, rejected the demand from the opposition leaders, and instead inquired whether they had made the same demands during Israel's previous military incursions in the Gaza Strip. She was presumably referring to Operation Cast Lead, when the Congress-led coalition was in power. Swaraj insisted that the government continued to support the Palestinian cause at international fora even as it condemned instances of cross-border rocket attacks directed against Israeli civilian centres.[89]

Defence Joint Ventures

Israeli companies have set up defence joint ventures with both the Indian state-owned as well as private sector companies to expand arenas of cooperation. (Please see Appendix). The Hindustan Aeronautics Limited (HAL) JV with Elbit, called HALBIT, was set up in 2007 to not just focus on maintenance of avionics, simulators and training systems procured from the Israeli company but also to collaborate in the design and development of such systems. HALBIT has products encompassing the areas of simulation, avionics, and computer-aided learning systems (CALS). State-owned Bharat Dynamics Limited (BDL), as pointed out earlier, is the lead integrator for the MRSAM and LRSAM missile systems, along with Rafael, Bharat Electronics Limited (BEL) and Larsen and Toubro (L&T).

India's private sector defence companies have entered into significant joint ventures with Israeli companies to address the requirements of the Indian armed forces. HELA Systems Private Limited, formed by Tatas with IAI's subsidiary, Elta Systems Ltd (74-24 per cent share), was set up in 2004 and has solutions in electronic warfare and homeland security, among other niche areas. The JV had a turnover of Rs. 54.2 crores in 2020-21.[90] Rafael Advanced Defence Systems Ltd.'s proposal for a JV with the Indian company, Mahindra and Mahindra in 2012 did not get regulatory approvals of the Foreign Investment Promotion Board (FIPB). As part of the JV, Rafael was to invest in the naval systems division of Mahindra and Mahindra in Pune.[91]

The JV between Adani Defence and Aerospace and Elbit Systems, meanwhile, set up an advanced UAV manufacturing facility in Hyderabad. The Adani group also signed a Letter of Award (LoA) with Elbit-ISTAR and Alpha Design Technologies Pvt Ltd in March 2016 to work together on UAVs for Indian requirements as well as for export opportunities.[92] The Adani-Elbit UAV Complex was inaugurated in December 2018.

The Adani-Elbit JV secured the distinction of supplying Indian-manufactured UAVs to an unnamed Southeast Asian country. Other reports had mentioned that the country in question was Philippines, and that the value of the deal was over $180 million, for a range of UAVs produced by Elbit, including Hermes 900, Hermes 450 for long-range missions and Skylark I and III for tactical missions.[93] Both Adani and Elbit agreed to set up a Design and Development Centre at Hyderabad in February 2020 to focus on co-developing defence technologies.[94]

The Adani Group has another JV with Israel Weapons Industries (IWI) through PLR (Precise, Lethal, Reliable) Systems Limited. The company in November 2021 secured an order from the MoD, for its Masada 9 mm pistols, for the Indian Navy's marine commandos (MARCOS). The Adani Group acquired a majority stake in September 2020 in PLR Systems, which itself was incorporated in 2013.[95] PLR Systems manufactures the Tavor assault rifles, the Galil sniper rifle, the Uzi sub-machine gun, among a host of niche products increasingly being used by the Indian armed forces and the central armed police forces (CAPF). The company is the first private sector entity to be given a license by the Government to manufacture small arms and ammunition.

Wipro Infrastructure Engineering (WIN), set up in 2013 by Wipro Enterprises, acquired an Israeli aerospace company, HR Givon in 2016, which manufactures metallic parts and assemblies for the aerospace industry. Wipro Aerospace has manufacturing sites in Israel, apart from India and the US. The IAI signed a Strategic Teaming Agreement with Wipro in July 2017—one of the four defence-related agreements signed by the Indian private sector during the visit of Prime Minister Modi to Israel.[96]

Apart from the Wipro-IAI agreement, other defence-related agreements that were signed by the private sector companies, at the first meeting of the India-Israel CEO Forum, included those between Mahindra Aerostructures and Elbit Systems, Mahindra Telephonics and Shachaf Engineering for strategic electronics, Kalyani Strategic Systems Limited and IAI for opportunities in air defence systems, radars, among others, and Dynamatic Technologies, Elcom Systems with the IAI for collaboration in the field of unmanned systems.[97]

Industry groups like the Society for Indian Defence Manufacturers (SIDM), along with SIBAT, the Israeli MoD defence cooperation directorate, have taken an active interest to build partnerships between Indian and Israeli defence firms. At a MoD, SIDM, SIBAT webinar in September 2020, Indian MoD officials flagged the country's huge modernization requirements relating to artillery guns, multi-role fighters, helicopters, among other equipment and the opportunities for cooperation between Indian and Israeli defence firms. It was pointed out during the event that at least nine Indian companies have signed 23 MoUs with four Israeli firms—IAI, Rafael, Elbit and Elta Systems.[98] Joint MoD-SIDM teams have also visited Israel to explore business opportunities.

Indian Defence and Aerospace Exports to Israel

Though minimal, India's defence and aerospace exports to Israel include helicopters, airframe structures, as well as arms and ammunition. Israel showed interest in the *Lakshya* pilotless aircraft and paid for demonstration flights but did not proceed with buying the aircraft.[99] A contract for one *Dhruv* helicopter was signed by the HAL with IAI in November 2004. An MOU for joint marketing of the *Dhruv* helicopter—integrated with IAI's avionics, was also signed, though not much progress was made on this front.

HAL's export business encompasses work packages, conversion kits, among others, for jet aircrafts. HAL secured a contract from the IAI in 2002 for the conversion of Boeing 737 passenger jets to cargo aircraft. This was HAL's first foray in the international civil aviation market.[100] HAL also bagged an order from IAI to make airframe structures for transport aircraft in 2018.[101]

India has exported arms and ammunition (HS Classification Code 93) to Israel to the tune of at least US$ 200 million, even as it has imported nearly US$ 80 million of goods under the same classification.[102] The Indian private sector is also engaging with Israeli companies and agencies to fulfill their security requirements. Tonbo Imaging, for instance, is a niche Start-Up that began eight years ago with Rs 220 crore of private capital and has generated revenue of Rs 400 crore. The CEO of the company, while speaking at a seminar on Atmanirbhar Bharat in February 2021, informed the audience that even the Israeli external intelligence agency, the Mossad, was one of his customers.[103] Earlier, in October 2016, the private sector company, Alpha Design Technologies bagged a multi-million dollar contract from Elbit Systems to supply VHF communication devices for exports.[104] As noted earlier, the Adani-Elbit UAV joint venture has exported UAV's to a Southeast Asian country.

The Atmanirbhar Bharat Abhiyan

The Ministry of Defence (MoD) is laying a lot of emphasis on defence indigenisation, domestic procurement and defence exports. During the period 2015–2021, over 60 per cent of capital procurement contracts of the MoD by number (190 out of 304) and 43 per cent by value (Rs 1,39,038 crore out of Rs 3,21,376 crore) were secured by the domestic industry.[105] The Government's Atmanirbhar Bharat Abhiyan (ABA) aims to unlock the potential of the domestic industry and manufacturers to meet the country's growing requirements. The ABA call has special significance for the defence sector, as the country has long been dependent on imports to fulfil most of its platform as well as niche equipment requirements.

To encourage innovation-led technology development in the defence and aerospace sector, the iDEX—Innovation for Defence Excellence, was launched in April 2018. Four Defence India Start-Up Challenges (DISC) have been held so far, in which over 1,000 Start-Ups have participated. Budgetary support of Rs 500 crore has been earmarked for iDEX till 2025–26, for Start-Ups, MSMEs and individual investors, through the Defence Innovation Organisation (DIO), an umbrella organisation formed with financial contributions from the aeronautics major, Hindustan Aeronautics Limited (HAL) and Bharat Electronics Limited (BEL).[106]

In the 2021–22 defence budget, an amount of Rs 1,000 crore has been exclusively earmarked for procurement from Start-Ups. The 2022-23 budget, meanwhile, set aside an allocation of 25 per cent of R&D budget for the academia, Start-Ups and the private industry. Over 80 Start-Ups are developing more than 30 cutting-edge products. The Government aims to double the number of products developed by Start-Ups to at least 60 by 2024. In order to more actively involve the stakeholders in developing cutting-edge products most suited to the requirements of the armed forces, iDEX4Fauji was also launched in September 2020.

The Strategic Partnership (SP) model, first promulgated as part of the Defence Procurement Procedure 2016, is an effort to energise the domestic defence industrial ecosystem. The model seeks to encourage domestic industry to enter into tie-ups with global original equipment manufacturers (OEMs) to set up manufacturing and infrastructure supply chains with transfer of technology (ToT). The Defence Acquisition Council (DAC) approved the issue of Request for Proposal (RfP) for construction of six conventional submarines, in June 2021, the first such project pursued under this model.

Up to forty-nine per cent foreign direct investment (FDI) is permitted through the automatic route while investment beyond that requires Government approval. The FDI limit was raised from 49 to 74 per cent in August 2020. The total FDI in the defence sector till January 2021 was Rs. 4,191 crore. It is pertinent to note that a significant portion of this, Rs. 2,871 crore, was received after 2014. The Government has approved 44 FDI proposals in the defence sector.[107]

The Government has introduced a separate domestic capital expenditure (CAPEX) budget of Rs 51,930 crore in 2020–21, nearly half of the total CAPEX budget. In 2021–22, this figure increased to Rs 71,438 crore, or 64 per cent of the total capital expenditure budget of Rs 1,11,463.21 crore.[108] In the 2022-23 defence budget, the domestic capital expenditure budget rose to

Rs. 84,598 crore, or nearly 68 per cent of the total capital budget of about Rs 125,000 crore.[109]

The Policy for Indigenisation of Components and Spares used in defence platforms, which was notified in March 2019, had actually suggested that this domestic CAPEX be increased by 15 per cent every year. The actual increase in 2021–22, which was close to 30 per cent, therefore, was double of that suggested. In August 2020, a 'positive' list of indigenisation, of 101 items, was released. The list included mostly major platforms like armoured fighting vehicles (AFVs), conventional submarines, light combat helicopters (LCHs), artillery guns and also items like radars. Going forward, the aim is to procure such items from the domestic industry, within specific periods, while embargoing their imports.

The second and the third lists were released in May 2021 and April 2022 respectively, comprising another 209 items including sensors, weapons and ammunition, radars, tank engines, AEW&C systems, which will only be sourced from the domestic industry by 2025.[110] Two indigenisation lists of sub-systems/components/assemblies were also released in December 2021 and March 2022, respectively. The DRDO also released a list of 108 systems and sub-systems in August 2020, which can be designed, developed and produced exclusively by the domestic industry.[111] The contract for 83 Light Combat Aircraft (LCA), valued at over Rs 48,000 crores, is the biggest domestic procurement contract ever. More than 500 MSMEs will be involved in executing the project.

India has also made rapid strides in defence exports. India was listed at the 23rd position as the global arms exporter by SIPRI in 2020, the first time that India made it to the list. The aim is to achieve a defence exports target of US$ 5 billion by 2025. With a strong domestic defence industry and a strong exports profile, India aims to become an essential part of the global defence value chain. At the same time, the aim is to reduce the country's dependence on defence imports. India has spent over US$ 36 billion (SIPRI TIV) on imports during 2010–20. Over 90 per cent of imports were from Russia (accounting for 63 per cent), the US (11 per cent), Israel (8 per cent), France (7.5 per cent) and the UK (3 per cent). During 2015–19, India accounted for more than 9 per cent of global arms imports. India's cumulative arms imports during 2016–20, though, were 33 per cent lower than the imports during 2011-15.

The Government therefore, has taken significant policy decisions in recent times to boost domestic defence manufacturing, facilitate defence indigenization, reduce imports and enhance exports. There is a robust intent and resolve on the part of the Government to make the Indian defence sector companies 'Vishwa Vyapi' (world-encompassing) companies.[112]

Srijan Defence Indigenization Portal

Given this policy framework, what will be the impact on India's key defence relationships with strategic partners like Israel? It is instructive to look at the Srijan defence indigenisation portal, which became active in August 2020.[113] The portal lists items which have been procured from foreign original equipment manufacturers (OEMs) by the DPSUs, ordnance factories and Service headquarters. The domestic industry is encouraged to engage and partner with the private sector in order to assist in the MoD's indigenization efforts. The domestic industry can either design, develop and produce these equipment on their own or through joint ventures with the OEMs.

The Srijan portal flows from the March 2019 Policy for the Indigenisation of Components and Spares used in Defence Platforms for DPSUs/OFBs. The Policy document notes that the value of components imported by the DPSUs/OFBs during 2017–18 was nearly Rs 14,000 crores. The aim is to reduce the import bill of the DPSUs on this count. The MoD specifically pledges to support the development of capabilities relating to engine technology, materials technology and electronic chip technology. It will also give priority to indigenized components for testing and evaluation and encourage their exports.[114]

More than 19,000 products, imported during the period 2018–22, have been listed for indigenization by the target year 2025–26. By July 2021, the Indian industry had shown interest for indigenization of nearly 3,000 items. The portal lists, as of end of January 2022, nearly 90 products worth Rs. 50 million (Rs. 5 crore) and above, which have been imported during 2020–21, for a cumulative value of Rs. 20,000 million (Rs 2,000 crores or about US$ 270 million).[115] These include components like data link transmitters, guided missile components and navigation instruments, imported by the Bharat Dynamics Limited (BDL), from Israeli OEMs like Elbit Systems and the Israel Aircraft Industries (IAI). The cumulative value of the imported components, from 2019 onwards and projected requirement till 2023, is close to Rs 1,000 million (Rs 100 crores or about US$ 14 million).

Earlier in September 2021, at least four such parts and equipment imported by the electronics major, Bharat Dynamics Limited (BDL) and the aerospace major, Hindustan Aeronautics Limited (HAL), from Israeli OEMs like Elbit Systems and the IAI, were listed. These include equipment for the beyond visual range (BVR) 'Astra' weapon system produced by the BDL, and display head assembly by HAL Avionics Division, Korwa. The cumulative value of imports of these equipment till 2025 is expected to be more than Rs. 1,300 million (Rs. 130 crore/US$ 18 million). The projected value of imports by HAL's Korwa unit from Israeli companies of products valued between Rs 10–50 million (Rs 1 crore–Rs 5 crore) till 2025 is expected be nearly Rs 700 million (Rs 70 crore/US$ 9 million). The projected value of imports by HAL's Korwa unit, apart from BDL, BEL and the HAL, from Israeli companies of products valued between Rs 0.5–5 million (Rs 0.05 crore–Rs 0.5 crore) up to 2025, is expected to be nearly Rs 138 million (Rs 13.8 crore/US$ 2 million).

Previously, the portal had also listed equipment and parts being imported from Israeli OEMs related to the Akash missile system (by BDL) and electronic and niche items by BDL and HAL. In September 2020, for instance, at least 23 products, worth over Rs 10 million (Rs 1 crore) each, were being sourced from Israeli companies. In September 2021, this number has reduced to eight. Items like the pressurised container system and sensor package unit for the Akash missile system made by the BDL, printed circuit boards and voltage control oscillators imported by the HAL, are no longer listed on the portal, perhaps signifying success in the indigenisation of such parts. In March 2016, Defence Minister Manohar Parrikar had informed Parliament that the imported content in the Akash missile system—touted as an indigenous system– was around 10 per cent.[116] If the BDL was no longer importing some parts for the Akash missile system, the imported components percentage would have surely come down.

The Srijan defence indigenisation portal, is therefore, a significant initiative which brings to attention the consequences of India's defence indigenisation efforts for key defence relationships. Going forward, the quantum of defence imports from Israel, of products and equipment currently being imported, will reduce to the tune of at least Rs 9,000 million (Rs 900 crores or about US$ 120 million), if the indigenisation efforts of the MoD in conjunction with the Indian industry, the DPSUs and ordnance factories, fructifies. Admittedly, this amount is not that significant in the current overall context and volume of the Indo-Israel defence trade, but is useful to highlight, given the MoD's robust indigenisation efforts. The cumulative impact of the policy measures that India is following in the defence sector to attain self-reliance and promote indigenization, if taken to their logical conclusion, will negatively impact the quantum of defence trade with key partners like Israel, less so in the near term but increasingly so in the medium-to-long terms.

Table 1: Annual Import Value of Equipment and Projected Requirement from Israeli OEMs (2017-26) Rs 10 million (approx. US$ 130,000) and Above

DPSU	*Imported product*	*Import Value of product (Rs in Million)*
AWEIL	Buffer recoil mechanism	91
	Barrel extension assembly	139.7
	Slide assembly retracting	60.6
	Cover assembly	129.4
	Plate assembly with safety	158.2
	Barrel machine gun	182.6
	Yaw Bearing Assembly	16.47
BEL	Electronic modem for ETC	701.2
	MFSTAR-Antenna	497
	Radio Interface Adapter for ETC	142.2
	Radio Interface card	60
	Monitor Sync Unit (MSU) Electronic module	45
	Yaw Bearing Assembly	16.47
BDL	Data link transfer for Astra launcher (Elbit systems)	330.7
	RF Front end (Astra) (Elbit Systems)	361.9
	Inertial measuring unit (Astra) (IAI Ltd)	703.9
	Sensor package unit	1015.7
	Ring laser gyro	535.2
	Pressurized missile container	637.5

DPSU	*Imported product*	*Import Value of product (Rs in Million)*
HAL	Display head assembly	320
	Radar processer	1077.7
	Transmitter	239.57
	Combiner assembly	261.77
	Beam Combiner	93.41
	Electronic components assembly	76.87
	Voltage control oscillator	60.21
	Portable solid state memory 64 GB Flash Disc Code	24.57
	Printed circuit board	42.1
	Electronic components assembly	97.9
	Electronic components assembly	15.57
	Radio Frequency Interference filter	14.84
	Filter box assembly	23.74
	Tilt motor	13.51
	Video/Audio Coder/Encoder	11.97
	Night vision goggle Gen 111	735
	Total import value	Rs 8933.47 million ($ 120 million approx)

Note: The Srijan portal maintains a dynamic list, where the parts and/or components are de-listed or categorized as 'indigenized'/'item not required', etc. depending on the status of indigenization. The items included in the table are those which the Srijan portal explicitly mentions were imported from Israeli OEMs.

Source: Ministry of Defence, 'Opportunities for Make in India Defence', Department of Defence Production, at https://srijandefence.gov.in/ProductList (Accessed September 2020, September 2021 and April 2022).

NOTES

1. N.A.K. Browne, 'A perspective on India-Israel defence and security ties', in Jayant Prasad and S. Samuel C. Rajiv (eds.) *India and Israel: The Making of a Strategic Partnership,* Routledge, London, 2020, pp. 15-25.
2. See, 'Transfers of major weapons: Deals with deliveries or orders made for 1992 to 2020', SIPRI Arms Transfers Database, at https://armstrade.sipri.org/armstrade/page/trade_register.php (Accessed August 24, 2021).
3. 'Eye in the sky to guard Gujarat coast', *The Times of India*, January 18, 2011, at http://articles.timesofindia.indiatimes.com/2011-01-18/ahmedabad/28352057_1_uav-squadron-unmanned-aerial-vehicle-squadron-western-coast (Accessed September 25, 2021).
4. Press Trust of India, 'Indian Navy commission's first UAV squadron', January 7, 2006, at https://us.rediff.com/news/2006/jan/06uav.htm?q=np&file=.htm (Accessed September 25, 2021).
5. Gary Mortimer, 'Navy Establishes Indian Third UAV Squadron in Tamil Nadu for Maritime Operations', April 10, 2012, at https://www.suasnews.com/2012/04/indian-navy-establishes-third-uav-squadron-in-tamil-nadu-for-maritime-operations/ (Accessed September 25, 2021).
6. 'India Buys 50 Herons in $500M IAI Deal', February 26, 2019, at https://www.uasvision.com/2019/02/26/india-buys-50-herons-in-500m-iai-deal/ (Accessed September 25, 2021).

7. Israel Aircraft Industries, 'Heron-TP', at https://www.iai.co.il/p/heron-tp (Accessed September 25, 2021).
8. Manu Pubby, 'Government approves $400-million plan to procure armed Heron TP drones from Israel', *The Economic Times*, July 14, 2018, at https://economictimes.indiatimes.com/news/defence/government-approves-400-million-plan-to-procure-armed-heron-tp-drones-from-israel/articleshow/48906195.cms?utm_source=contentofinterest&utm _medium = text&utm_campaign=cppst (Accessed September 25, 2021).
9. Snehesh Alex Philip, 'Indian Army will soon get 4 Heron TP drones on lease from Israel, plans to deploy them at LAC', *The Print*, May 26, 2021, at https://theprint.in/defence/indian-army-will-soon-get-4-heron-tp-drones-on-lease-from-israel-plans-to-deploy-them-at-lac/665981/ (Accessed September 25, 2021).
10. 'Army receives four new Israeli Heron drones: How these UAVs will boost India's surveillance capabilities in Ladakh,' *Times Now Digital*, December 1, 2021, at https://www.times now news.com/india/article/army-receives-four-new-israeli-heron-drones-how-these-uavs-will-boost-indias-surveillance-capabilities-in-ladakh/836868 (Accessed February 10, 2022).
11.. Israel Aircraft Industries, 'Leasing – A Flexible Approach to UAS Operations', June 7, 2021, at https://www.iai.co.il/news-media/features/uas-leasing (Accessed September 25, 2021).
12. Snehesh Alex Philip, 'Project Cheetah set to take off, India to get upgraded & armed drones from Israel', *The Print*, August 3, 2021, at https://theprint.in/defence/project-cheetah-set-to-take-off-india-to-get-upgraded-armed-drones-from-israel/708122/ (Accessed September 25, 2021).
13. Hindustan Aeronautics Limited, *Annual Report 2019-20*, p. 4, at https://hal-india.co.in/Common/Uploads/Finance/HAL_AR-2019-20%20Final.pdf (Accessed September 25, 2021).
14. Rajya Sabha, 'Delay in delivery if aircrafts by Israel', Unstarred Question Number 4347, May 5, 2010, at https://pqars.nic.in/annex/219/Au4347.pdf (Accessed September 25, 2021).
15. The DRDO and the IAF began the project to develop an AEW&C aircraft indigenously, in 2004. Embraer-145 was the chosen aircraft to mount the indigenously developed radar. M.S. Eswaran, the head of the Centre for Airborne Systems (CABS)—which began life as the Airborne Surveillance Warning and Control Centre (ASWAC) in 1985—writes that the proposal by the DRDO to develop an indigenous system was cleared by the Cabinet Committee on Security (CCS) within a week after it was submitted. '*Netra*: The Indigenous Airborne Early Warning and Control System', *Technology Focus*, 29 (2), p. 3, at https://www.drdo.gov.in/sites/default/files/technology-focus-documrnt/TF_April_2021.pdf (Accessed September 25, 2021).
16. The Comptroller and Auditor General (CAG), though, has flagged inconsistencies in the selection of the Embraer aircraft by the DRDO and the IAF, given that it cannot operate from higher altitudes in places like Ladakh, as well as for not ostensibly fulfilling significant operational requirements of the IAF. See Pradip R Sagar, 'How a CAG report exposed DRDO's mishandling of AEW&CS programme', August 29, 2018, at https://www.theweek.in/news/india/2018/08/29/How-a-CAG-report-exposed-DRDO-mishandling-of-AEW-CS-programme.html (Accessed September 25, 2021).
17. '*Netra*: The Indigenous Airborne Early Warning and Control System', *Technology Focus*, p. 4; See also Sandeep Unnithan, 'Made in India monitoring device helped IAF keep tap on Pakistan jets' movement during airstrike in Balakot', *India Today*, February 27, 2019, at https://www.indiatoday.in/india/story/airborne-early-warning-and-control-iaf-pakistan-jets-movement-airstrike balakot 1465935-2019-02-27 (Accessed September 25, 2021).
18. Rajat Pandit, 'India plans major indigenous project for six powerful "eyes in the sky" AWACS', *The Times of India*, December 16, 2020, at http://timesofindia.indiatimes.com/articleshow/

79766365.cms?utm_source=contentofinterest&utm_medium=text&utm_campaign=cppst (Accessed September 25, 2021); Snehesh Alex Philip, 'Govt sanctions 6 new "eyes in the sky" worth Rs 10,994 crore for Air Force', *The Print*, December 17, 2020, at https://theprint.in/defence/govt-sanctions-6-new-eyes-in-the-sky-worth-rs-10994-crore-for-air-force/568871/ (Accessed September 25, 2021).

19. Neelam Mathews, 'India wants long-endurance AWACS', April 10, 2014, at https://www.ainonline.com/aviation-news/defense/2014-04-10/india-wants-long-endurance-awacs (Accessed September 25, 2021).
20. Snehesh Alex Philip, 'Modi govt okays 6 more "eyes in the sky" for IAF, DRDO project to cost Rs 11,000 crore', September 9, 2021, at Modi govt okays 6 more 'eyes in the sky' for IAF, DRDO project to cost Rs 11,000 crore (msn.com) (Accessed September 25, 2021).
21. P.K. Chakravorty, 'Gunners Day and the Way Ahead', October 2013, at https://www.indiastrategic.in/topstories3060_Gunners_Day_way_ahead.htm (Accessed September 25, 2021).
22. Ministry of Defence, *Annual Report 2010-11,* p. 25, at https://www.mod.gov.in/dod/sites/default/files/AR-eng-2011.pdf (Accessed September 25, 2021).
23. Ajai Shukla, 'With cutting-edge AESA radar, Jaguar is IAF's first fighter', *The Business Standard*, May 25, 2018, at https://www.business-standard.com/article/economy-policy/with-cutting-edge-aesa-radar-jaguar-is-iaf-s-first-fighter-118052500033_1.html (Accessed September 25, 2021).
24. *Annual Report 2015-16*, Aeronautical Development Agency, p. 21, at https://www.ada.gov.in/images/Annual%20Report%202015-16.pdf (Accessed September 25, 2021).
25. Ajai Shukla, 'Cutting-edge Israeli radar wins air force approval for Tejas fighter', *Business Standard*, October 25, 2015, at https://www.business-standard.com/article/economy-policy/cutting-edge-israeli-radar-wins-air-force-approval-for-tejas-fighter-115102500749_1.html (Accessed September 25, 2021).
26. When one of these radars was involved in an accident in May 2009, the CAG criticized lax maintenance protocols, which cost over Rs. 300 crores to repair. Comptroller and Auditor General of India, Report No. 20 of 2011-12 (Air Force and Navy), pp. 27-31, at https://cag.gov.in/cag_old/sites/default/files/audit_report_files/Union_Compliance_ Defence_ Air_Force_and_Navy_20_2011.pdf (Accessed September 30, 2021)
27. M Anantha Krishnan, 'DRDO Kicks off Mission to Develop Surveillance Airship', January 1, 2014, at https://www.newindianexpress.com/nation/2014/jan/01/DRDO-Kicks-off-Mission-to-Develop-Surveillance-Airship-558257.html (Accessed September 30, 2021)
28. Public Accounts Committee, 'Avoidable procurement of a mobile nitrogen gas generation plant, Infructuous procurement of material, Development of integrated aerostat surveillance system, and Irregular expenditure on vehicle testing ground', Action Taken Report by the Government on the Observations/Recommendations of the Committee contained in their One Hundred and Thirty First Report, Sixteenth Lok Sabha, Ministry of Defence, September 2020, pp. 5-18, at http://164.100.47.193/lsscommittee/Public%20Accounts/17_Public_Accounts_20.pdf (Accessed September 30, 2021).
29. Arvind Chauhan, 'DRDO's Agra lab spends Rs 49.50 cr, 6 yrs, in developing surveillance system which fails Army standards', July 24, 2017, at https://timesofindia.indiatimes.com/city/agra/drdos-agra-lab-spends-rs-49-50-cr-6-yrs-in-developing-surveillance-system-which-fails-army-standards/articleshow/59732675.cms (Accessed September 30, 2021).
30. Vijay Mohan, 'IAF to procure 8 aerostat radars', February 3, 2016, at https://

www.tribuneindia.com/news/archive/nation/iaf-to-procure-8-aerostat-radars-191264 (Accessed September 30, 2021).

31. Ministry of Defence, *Annual Report 2017-18,* p. 82.
32. Indian Navy, 'Successful Conduct of LR SAM Firing by Indian Navy', December 2015, at https://indiannavy.nic.in/content/successful-conduct-lr-sam-firing-indian-navy (Accessed September 30, 2021).
33. Ministry of Defence, *Annual Report 2018-19,* p. 97, at https://www.mod.gov.in/sites/default/files/MoDAR2018.pdf (Accessed September 30, 2021).
34. Press Information Bureau, 'Flag off ceremony of final production batch of LRSAM Missiles', February 14, 2021, at https://www.pib.gov.in/PressReleasePage.aspx?PRID=1697942 (Accessed September 30, 2021).
35. Seth Frantzman, 'Israel and India test MRSAM air defense system', *Defence News,* January 5, 2021, at https://www.defensenews.com/training-sim/2021/01/05/israel-and-india-test-of-mrsam-air-defense-system/ (Accessed September 30, 2021).
36. Lok Sabha, 'Acquisition of missiles from Israel', Unstarred Question No. 2819, March 13, 2015, at http://loksabhaph.nic.in/Questions/QResult15.aspx?qref=13180&lsno=16 (Accessed September 30, 2021).
37. 'Procurement of missiles for Barak systems cleared', *The Indian Express,* December 24, 2013, at https://indianexpress.com/article/news-archive/web/procurement-of-missiles-for-barak-systems-cleared/ (Accessed September 30, 2021).
38. Manu Pubby, 'Israeli firms IAI, Rafael taken off restricted list after closure of corruption case', *The Print,* April 5, 2018, at https://theprint.in/defence/israeli-firms-iai-rafael-taken-off-restricted-list-after-closure-of-corruption-case/47393/ (Accessed September 30, 2021); Vivek Raghuvanshi, 'India lifts blacklisting for two Israel defense companies', *Defense News,* April 13, 2018, at https://www.defensenews.com/global/mideast-africa/2018/04/12/india-lifts-blacklisting-for-two-israel-defense-companies/ (Accessed September 30, 2021).
39. Sushant Singh, 'Ministry of Defence scraps $500 million Israeli missile deal, wants DRDO to make in India', November 20, 2017, at https://indianexpress.com/article/india/ministry-of-defence-scraps-500-million-israeli-missile-deal-wants-drdo-to-make-in-india-4945571/ (Accessed October 2, 2021).
40. Rajat Pandit, 'Critically short of anti-tank missiles, Army sounds alarm', January 28, 2018, at http://timesofindia.indiatimes.com/articleshow/62678079.cms?utm_source= contentof interest &utm_medium=text&utm_campaign=cppst (Accessed October 2, 2021).
41. Lok Sabha, 'Shortage of anti-tank missiles', Unstarred Question 2035, March 7, 2018, at http://loksabhaph.nic.in/Questions/QResult15.aspx?qref=63502&lsno=16 (Accessed October 2, 2021).
42. Neelam Mathews, 'US offers four new defence projects to India', January 29, 2015, at https://www.ainonline.com/aviation-news/defense/2015-01-29/us-offers-four-new-defense-projects-india (Accessed October 2, 2021).
43. 'Compliance Audit on Army and Ordnance and Factories, Union Government, Defence Services', Comptroller and Auditor General of India, August 6, 2010, at https://cag.gov.in/cag_old/content/report-no-12-2010-compliance-audit-army-and-ordnance-and-factories-union-government-defence (Accessed October 2, 2021).
44. 'Nag anti-tank missile back in reckoning', July 12, 2008, at http://timesofindia.indiatimes.com/articleshow/3225233.cms?utm_source=contentofinterest&utm_ medium= text&utm_campaign=cppst (Accessed October 2, 2021).
45. Pradip R. Sagar, 'Defence Deal with Israel Hits a Roadblock', June 5, 2015, at http://

www.newindianexpress.com/nation/Defence-Deal-With-Israel-Hits-a-Roadblock/2015/06/05/article2850156.ece (Accessed October 2, 2021).
46. Rajya Sabha, 'Scrapping of Spike Anti-Tank Guided Missiles Deal', Starred Question No. 24, February 5, 2018, at https://rajyasabha.nic.in/rsnew/Questions/QResult.aspx (Accessed October 2, 2021).
47. Malavika Velayinikal, 'Guided missiles homing in with Indian deep tech', *Mint*, February 15, 2021, at https://www.livemint.com/news/business-of-life/guided-missiles-homing-in-with-indian-deep-tech-11613314273154.htm (Accessed October 2, 2021).
48. Press Trust of India, 'HAL signs agreement with Israel's Elbit Systems for DOHS supply', February 8, 2021, at https://www.hindustantimes.com/business/hal-signs-agreement-with-israel-s-elbit-systems-for-dohs-supply-101612782225898.html (Accessed October 4, 2021).
49. Ministry of Defence, *Annual Report 2004-05*, New Delhi, p. 75.
50. Rajya Sabha, 'Weapons from Israel', Unstarred Question 1790, August 10, 2005, at https://rajyasabha.nic.in/rsnew/Questions/QResult.aspx (Accessed October 4, 2021).
51. Rahul Bedi, 'Spooked By Ladakh Standoff, India Signs $200m Deal for Israeli SPICE Bombs', December 26, 2020, at https://thewire.in/security/india-200-million-dollar-deal-israel-spice-bombs (Accessed October 4, 2021).
52. Rahul Singh, 'Indian firm edges out Israeli rival, set to upgrade army's AK-47s', November 1, 2021, at https://www.hindustantimes.com/india-news/indian-firm-edges-out-israeli-rival-set-to-upgrade-army-s-ak47s-101635702384964.html (Accessed November 5, 2021).
53. Rahul Singh, 'Private sector firm set to make small arms', *The Hindustan Times*, November 2, 2021, at https://www.hindustantimes.com/india-news/private-sector-firm-set-to-make-small-arms-101635814498850.html (Accessed November 5, 2021).
54. Ministry of External Affairs, '16th round of India-Israel foreign office consultations', Ministry of External Affairs, December 7, 2020, at https://mea.gov.in/press-releases.htm?dtl/33261/16th+round+of+indiaisrael+foreign+office+consultations (Accessed October 5, 2021).
55. Press Information Bureau, '15th India-Israel Joint Working Group meeting in Tel Aviv', October 29, 2021, at https://pib.gov.in/PressReleasePage.aspx?PRID=1767593 (Accessed October 30, 2021).
56. N.A.K. Browne, 'A Perspective on India-Israel Defence and Security Ties', in Jayant Prasad and S. Samuel C. Rajiv (eds.) *India and Israel: The Making of a Strategic Partnership,* Routledge, London, 2020, p. 22.
57. Prakash Gopal, 'India-Israel Defence Engagement: A Naval Perspective', in Jayant Prasad and S. Samuel C. Rajiv (eds.), *India and Israel: The Making of a Strategic Partnership*, pp. 77-83.
58. Rajya Sabha, 'Installation of electronic surveillance system on Coco Island by China', May 27, 1998, at https://rajyasabha.nic.in/rsnew/Questions/QResult.aspx (Accessed October 10, 2021).
59. Philip, 'Govt sanctions 6 new "eyes in the sky" worth Rs 10,994 crore for Air Force', n. 18.
60. Rajya Sabha, 'Desertion of AWACS programme', Unstarred Question 2742, March 21, 2001, at https://pqars.nic.in/annex/192/Au2742.pdf (Accessed October 10, 2021).
61. Rajya Sabha, 'Projects delayed because of developing indigenous technology', Unstarred Question 3373, April 26, 2000, at https://pqars.nic.in/annex/189/Au3373.pdf (Accessed October 10, 2021).
62. Rajya Sabha, 'Purchase of pilotless planes from Israel', Question No. 1867, August 9, 2000, at https://pqars.nic.in/annex/190/Au1867.pdf https://pqars.nic.in/annex/189/Au3373.pdf (Accessed October 10, 2021).
63. Rajya Sabha, 'Achievements made by the DRDO', Unstarred Question No. 68, March 8, 2016, at https://rajyasabha.nic.in/rsnew/Questions/QResult.aspx (Accessed October 10, 2021).

64. Comptroller and Auditor General, 'Press release of Audit Report No. 13 of 2018 on Defence Services (Army)', August 2018, at http://14.143.90.243/cag_revamp/uploads/PressRelease/PR-Press-13-of-2018-1-05f5f6fb85a2021-47277784.pdf (Accessed October 10, 2021); Ministry of Defence, *Annual Report 2018-19*, p. 266, at https://www.mod.gov.in/sites/default/files/MoDAR2018.pdf (Accessed October 10, 2021).
65. Ibid.
66. Greg Waldron, 'IAI in MOU with Indian firms on local UAV production', February 5, 2020, at https://www.flightglobal.com/defence/iai-in-mou-with-indian-firms-on-local-uav-production/136542.article (Accessed October 10, 2021).
67. Comptroller and Auditor General, 'Report of the Comptroller and Auditor General of India for the year ended March 2014, Union Government (Defence Services), Air Force, No. 38 of 2015', at https://cag.gov.in/uploads/download_audit_report/2015/Union_Compliance_Defence_ Air_Force_Report_38_2015_annexures.pdf (Accessed October 10, 2021).
68. T.V. Parasuram, 'US unlikely to take early decision on Arrow sale to India', July 24, 2002, at https://www.outlookindia.com/newswire/story/us-unlikely-to-take-early-decision-on-arrow-sale-to-india/71206 (Accessed October 10, 2021).
69. Sanjay Badri-Maharaj, 'Ballistic missile defence for India', July 2, 2009, at http://www.bharat-rakshak.com/IAF/today/contemporary/328-bmd.html#gsc.tab=0 (Accessed October 10, 2021).
70. Manu Pubby, 'Sanctions could hit deliveries of S-400, AK 203 and 11356 frigates from Russia', *The Economic Times*, February 25, 2022, at https://economictimes.indiatimes.com/news/defence/sanctions-could-hit-deliveries-of-s-400-ak-203-and-11356-frigates-from-russia/articleshow/89814071.cms?utm_source=contentofinterest&utm_ medium= text&utm _ campaign=cppst (Accessed February 28, 2022).
71. See 'IAI Phalcon 707', Global Security.org, at https://www.globalsecurity.org/military/world/israel/phalcon.htm (Accessed October 20, 2021); See also Gareth Evans, 'Sixth sense: Asia's race for early warning missile detection capabilities', *Airforce Technology*, November 28, 2012, at https://www.airforce-technology.com/features/featurenorth-korea-missile-launch-warning-detection/ (Accessed October 20, 2021).
72. Rajya Sabha, 'Procurement of surveillance system from Israel', Unstarred Question No. 1098, August 2, 2000, at https://pqars.nic.in/annex/190/Au1098.pdf (Accessed October 25, 2021).
73. Rajya Sabha, 'Induction of AWACS', Unstarred Question 5487, May 17, 2000, at https://pqars.nic.in/annex/189/Au5487.pdf (Accessed October 25, 2021).
74. 'DRDO offers India Netra AEW&C on new platform', April 4, 2019, at https://www.defenseworld.net/news/24556/DRDO_Offers_India_Netra_ AEW_ C_ On_ New_Platform#.YSZSXo4zbIU (Accessed October 25, 2021).
75. Ajai Shukla, 'Israeli firm Elbit Systems offers to build 70 per cent of artillery guns in India', *Business Standard*, December 10, 2020, at https://www.business-standard.com/article/current-affairs/israeli-firm-elbit-systems-offers-to-build-70-of-artillery-guns-in-india-120120901372_1.html (Accessed October 25, 2021); Snehesh Alex Philip, 'Israel's ATHOS gun system or Atmanirbhar ATAGS? Defence negative list to finalise next week', *The Print*, May 28, 2021, at https://theprint.in/defence/israels-athos-gun-system-or-atmanirbhar-atags-defence-negative-list-to-finalise-next-week/666695/ (Accessed October 25, 2021).
76. Sandeep Unnithan, 'What's behind a massive order for Made-in-India howitzers', *India Today*, January 23, 2022, at https://www.indiatoday.in/india-today-insight/story/what-s-behind-a-massive-order-for-made-in-india-howitzers-1903375-2022-01-23 (Accessed January 30, 2022).
77. 'Israel Aerospace Industries Marks Most Profitable Year in Company History', Israel Aircraft Industries, March 16, 2022, at https://www.iai.co.il/annual-financial-2021#:~:text=The%20

Company's%20revenues%20in%202021,USD%20293%20million%20(approx. (Accessed April 30, 2022).

78. 'Rafael concludes FY 2021 with net profit of $133 million', IsraelDefense, April 4, 2022, at https://www.israeldefense.co.il/en/node/54120 (Accessed May 5, 2022); Rafael Advanced Defence Systems Limited, 'Rafael concludes FY 2020 with sales of $2.7 billion and net profit of $94 million', March 24, 2021, at https://www.rafael.co.il/press/rafael-concludes-fy-2020-with-sales-of-2-7-billion-and-net-profit-of-94-million/ (Accessed September 25, 2021).
79. Gili Cohen, 'Israel Is World's Largest Exporter of Drones, Study Finds', *Haaretz*, May 19, 2013, at https://www.haaretz.com/.premium-israel-is-greatest-exporter-of-drones-1.5243373 (Accessed September 25, 2021).
80. Royal United Services Institution, 'Armed drones in the Middle East', at https://drones.rusi.org/countries/israel/ (Accessed September 30, 2021).
81. Arie Egozi, 'Israeli Industry Pushing Jerusalem to Drop MTCR Drone Export Restrictions', September 27, 2021, at https://breakingdefense.com/2021/09/israeli-industry-pushing-jerusalem-to-drop-mtcr-drone-export-restrictions/ (Accessed September 30, 2021).
82. Rajya Sabha, 'Contracts for defence equipments with Israel', Unstarred Question No. 1093, November 28, 2001, at https://rajyasabha.nic.in/rsnew/Questions/QResult.aspx (Accessed October 2, 2021).
83. Lok Sabha, 'Indo-Israel Defence Deal', Unstarred Question No. 1382, November 27, 2007, http://loksabhaph.nic.in/Questions/QResult15.aspx?qref=56366&lsno=14 (Accessed October 2, 2021).
84. Rajya Sabha, 'Purchase of missiles from Israel', Unstarred Question No. 1108, August 22, 2007, at https://rajyasabha.nic.in/rsnew/Questions/QResult.aspx (Accessed October 2, 2021).
85. Rajya Sabha, 'Joint development programme with Israel to develop Iron Dome', Unstarred Question No. 2514, March 20, 2013, at https://rajyasabha.nic.in/rsnew/Questions/QResult.aspx (Accessed October 2, 2021).
86. Lok Sabha, 'Defence purchases from Israel', Unstarred Question No. 2189, December 5, 2014, at http://loksabhaph.nic.in/Questions/QResult15.aspx?qref=8695&lsno=16 (Accessed October 2, 2021).
87. 'Movement to Boycott Israeli Industry Hails India's Decision to Scrap $500m Missile Deal', *The Wire*, November 22, 2007, at https://thewire.in/diplomacy/bds-movement-israel-india-missile-deal (Accessed October 4, 2021).
88. Rajya Sabha, 'Uncorrected Verbatim Debates', Session 232, July 21, 2014, at https://rajyasabha.nic.in/business/newshow.aspx (Accessed September 10, 2021).
89. Ibid.
90. HELA Systems Private Limited, *Annual Report 2021*, at https://www.hela.in/HELA-Form-MGT-7.pdf (Accessed October 6, 2021).
91. Amrita Nair Ghaswalla, 'M&M wants to know why its plan for joint venture with Rafael was rejected', *The Hindu Business Line*, January 1, 2013, at https://www.thehindubusinessline.com/companies/MampM-wants-to-know-why-its-plan-for-joint-venture-with-Rafael-was-rejected/article20560520.ece (Accessed October 8, 2021).
92. Adani Enterprises, 'Adani Forays Into Defence Signs IoA With Elbit ISTAR And Alpha Design Technologies Pvt Ltd', March 30, 2016, at https://www.adanienterprises.com/newsroom/media-releases/Adani-forays-into-defence-signs-IoA-with-Elbit-ISTAR-and-Alpha-Design-Technologies-Pvt-Ltd (Accessed October 8, 2021).
93. Manu Pubby, 'Defence Expo 2020: Adani-Elbit JV exports India-made military drone', February 7, 2020, at https://economictimes.indiatimes.com/news/defence/defence-expo-2020-adani-

elbit-jv-exports-india-made-military-drone/articleshow/73998264.cms?from=mdr (Accessed October 8, 2021); 'Indo-Israeli UAV Joint Venture in $180 Million Export Deal with Philippines', *DefenseWorld*, June 15, 2019, at https://www.defenseworld.net/news/24957/Indo_Israeli_UAV_Joint_Venture_in__180_Million_Export_Deal_with_Philippines#.YYe9b2BBzIU (Accessed October 8, 2021).

94. Adani Defence, 'Adani-Elbit JV Further Steps up Their Presence in the International Markets', February 6, 2020, at https://www.adanidefence.com/newsroom/media-release/Adani-Elbit-JV-further-steps-up-their-presence-in-the-international-markets (Accessed October 8, 2021).
95. 'Adani's defence subsidiary acquires majority stake in PLR Systems', *Business Standard*, September 11, 2020, at https://www.business-standard.com/article/companies/adani-defence-subsidiary-acquires-majority-stake-in-plr-systems-120091101525_1.html (Accessed October 8, 2021).
96. Israel Aerospace Industries, 'Israel Aerospace Industries Signs a Strategic Teaming Agreement for Industrial Cooperation in the Production of Composite Aero Structures With Wipro Enterprises (P) Limited in India', July 5, 2017, at https://www.iai.co.il/israel-aerospace-industries-signs-strategic-teaming-agreement-industrial-cooperation-production (Accessed October 8, 2021).
97. Federation of Indian Chambers of Commerce and Industry, 'First Meeting of India-Israel CEOs Forum coincides with the visit of PM Modi to Israel', July 6, 2017, at https://ficci.in/PressRelease/2818/ficci-press-release-jul6-mou-israel1.pdf (Accessed October 9, 2021).
98. Ajai Shukla, 'India invites Israeli firms to cooperate in meeting $130 billion weapons need', *Business Standard*, September 25, 2021, at https://www.ajaishukla.com/2020/09/india-invites-israeli-firms-to.html (Accessed October 9, 2021).
99. Rajya Sabha, 'Sale of pilotless target aircraft Lakshya to Israel', Unstarred Question No. 2015, August 9, 2001, at https://rajyasabha.nic.in/rsnew/Questions/QResult.aspx (Accessed October 9, 2021).
100. 'HAL to outsource aircraft components to pvt. sector', *Rediff*, February 21, 2002, at https://m.rediff.com/money/2002/feb/21hal.htm (Accessed October 9, 2021).
101. Press Trust of India, 'HAL inks major deals with Israeli defence firms', July 19, 2006, at https://economictimes.indiatimes.com/industry/transportation/airlines-/-aviation/hal-inks-major-deals-with-israeli-defence-firms/articleshow/1778664.cms?utm_source=contentofinterest&utm_ medium=text&utm_campaign=cppst (Accessed October 9, 2021).
102. Ministry of Commerce and Industry, 'Export Import Data Bank', at https://tradestat.commerce.gov.in/eidb/default.asp (Accessed October 9, 2021).
103. Remarks by Arvind Laxmi Kumar, CEO, Tonbo Imaging, at the MoD-Industry Webinar on Budget 2021-2022, 'Galvanizing Efforts for Atmanirbar Bharat', New Delhi, February 23, 2021.
104. Alpha Design Technologies Limited, 'Alpha Design Technologies bags prestigious contract for defence communication equipment from Elbit Systems', October 6, 2016, at https://www.adtl.co.in/news/alpha-design-technologies-bags-prestigious-contract-for-defence-communication-equipment-from-elbit-systems (Accessed October 9, 2021).
105. Press Information Bureau, 'Government Spending on Military Modernisation', Ministry of Defence, Government of India, 8 March 2021, at https://pib.gov.in/PressReleseDetailm.aspx?PRID=1703203 (Accessed August 25, 2021).
106. Press Information Bureau, 'Innovations for Defence Excellence (iDEX)', Ministry of Defence, Government of India, July 28, 2021, at https://pib.gov.in/PressReleaseIframePage.aspx?PRID=1739954 (Accessed August 25, 2021); Press Information Bureau, "Defence Start-Ups', Ministry

of Defence, Government of India, December 17, 2021, at https://pib.gov.in/PressReleasePage.aspx?PRID=1782604 (Accessed December 25, 2021).

107. 'Government Spending on Military Modernisation', n. 105.
108. Press Information Bureau, 'Efforts to Encourage Domestic Manufacturing', Ministry of Defence, Government of India, August 2, 2021, at https://pib.gov.in/PressReleasePage.aspx?PRID=1741475 (Accessed August 10, 2021).
109. Press Information Bureau, 'Union Budget 2022-23', February 1, 2022, at https://www.pib.gov.in/PressReleasePage.aspx?PRID=1794415 (Accessed February 2, 2022).
110. Press Information Bureau, 'MoD Notifies "Second Positive Indigenisation List" of 108 Items to Promote Self-reliance and Defence Exports', Ministry of Defence, Government of India, May 31, 2021, at https://pib.gov.in/PressReleasePage.aspx?PRID=1723148 (Accessed July 10, 2021); Press Information Bureau, 'Production of Defence Products', August 5, 2022, at https://pib.gov.in/PressReleseDetailm.aspx?PRID=1848670 (Accessed August 30, 2022).
111. 'DRDO Comes Out With List of 108 Military Systems for Production by Domestic Industry', *The Economic Times*, August 24, 2020, at https://economictimes.indiatimes.com/news/defence/drdo-comes-out-with-list-of-108-military-systems-for-production-by-domestic-industry/articleshow/77726251.cms?utm_source=contentofinterest&utm _medium= text&utm _campaign=cppst (Accessed August 30, 2021).
112. Raksha Mantri Rajnath Singh used this term while speaking at a MoD-Industry webinar on the Defence Budget 2021–22, 'Galvanising Efforts for Atma Nirbhar Bharat', held at New Delhi, on February 23, 2021.
113. Ministry of Defence, 'Opportunities for Make in India in Defence', Department of Defence Production, at https://srijandefence.gov.in/ (Accessed February 2, 2022).
114. Ministry of Defence, 'Policy for Indigenization of Spares and Components used in Defence Platforms for DPSUs/OFBs', Department of Defence Production, March 8, 2019, at https://srijandefence.gov.in/Policy&framwork.pdf (Accessed February 2, 2022).
115. For reference purposes, 1 US$ is taken as equivalent to Rs 75. The portal lists the values of the components in Rs million.
116. Rajya Sabha, 'Achievements Made by DRDO', Unstarred Question No. 1168, March 8, 2016, at https://rajyasabha.nic.in/rsnew/Questions/QResult.aspx (Accessed August 25, 2021).

3

Internal Security and Border Security Cooperation

India and Israel have established significant cooperation mechanisms in border security and internal security. Israel's counter-terror policies and practices are a subject of much study and appreciation, especially by those who advocate the replication of similar 'muscular' policies to deal with terror threats. The chapter highlights key aspects of cooperation between India and Israel in border security and counter-terrorism.

Israel and Counter-terrorism

Israel's unique counter-terrorism experience is often touted as an important national attribute, which can be adapted to suit the requirements of other countries in their fight against terror. Israeli analysts note that the country has suffered more from terrorism than any other country in the world, in terms of the size of its population. The country's geography also imposes a unique vulnerability on its security choices. While terrorist incidents affect a narrow section of the population or territory in most other countries, in Israel, terrorism is viewed as a national security problem impacting the entire territory and population.

Till the 1973 Yom Kippur War, Israel's main concerns related to the need to repulse a joint conventional attack by its Arab enemies. The fledgling Israel

Defense Force (IDF) – termed the 'Israel Offense Force' in reality, by the former Vice Chief of the IDF, Gen. Israel Tal, successfully repulsed the Arab onslaught and protected the country's sovereignty during the 1948 War of Independence.[1] The 1948 War of Independence led to the establishment of the 'Green Line', demarcating the country's borders from its Arab neighbours. After the 1967 war, Israel occupied East Jerusalem, Golan Heights, Sinai, and the West Bank, territories beyond the Green Line. Israel, therefore, acquired strategic depth and pushed Syria out of its artillery range.

After the 1973 war, most of the significant threats that Israel had to grapple with frequently were asymmetric in nature. Organizations like the military wing of the Hamas, the Palestinian Islamic Jihad, the Popular Resistance Committees (PRC), among others, draw their ideological and physical sustenance from the long-running Israel-Palestinian conflict, described as a 'protracted' conflict four decades ago and which still continues unabated.[2]

The uprising (Intifada) by the Palestinians during the 1980s and the 2000s was a unique national security problem, initially viewed as a law-and-order problem but increasingly dealt with by the IDF, which was called to quell the violent protests.[3] These protests were accompanied by suicide bombings and increasing Israeli casualty figures. In the past two decades, until mid-2021, 1,377 Israeli citizens and 75 IDF soldiers, lost their lives as a result of acts of terrorism by Palestinian groups.[4] A majority of these fatalities have been due to suicide bombings. Israel has used a plethora of offensive and defensive kinetic measures (in terms of tactics) and active and passive defences to counter the asymmetric terror threats. Targeting the terrorist leadership, in preventive decapitating strikes, for instance, has been a hallmark of the Israeli counter-terror strategy. Israel has taken out key terrorist leaders, both within the Gaza Strip as well as in places like Dubai. In the military confrontations in the Gaza Strip – Operation Cast Lead (2008-09), Operation Pillar of Defence (2012), Operation Protective Edge (2014), Operation Guardian of the Walls (2021) – Israel has invested its effort in specifically targeting terrorist leadership as well as the terror infrastructure, beyond the Gaza Strip as well.

Israel, for instance, has carried out punitive strikes in places as far away as Iraq and Syria against both terror infrastructure and weapons storage sites and convoys that were allegedly supplying to groups like the Hamas and the

Hezbollah. Israel's military interventions in the Gaza Strip, post the 2005 disengagement, have been termed as a 'mowing the grass' tactics, in order to degrade enemy military capability. Israeli analysts, therefore, argue that such wars of attrition are not meant to achieve 'impossible political goals', in the face of intransigent Palestinian abilities to make compromises from their core positions on Israeli sovereignty and territoriality.[5]

As for active measures, the effective Iron Dome missile system is a unique example of the success of Israel's efforts to counter rapidly changing terror tactics. When the Palestinian terror groups indulged in suicide bombings, Israel built very effective barriers to prevent the entry of the suicide bombers into Israeli territory. When the Palestinian terror groups indulged in rocket attacks, primarily in order to overcome effective Israeli border security tactics, they were met with very effective measures like the Iron Dome point defence system.

The Iron Dome system, in operation since April 2011, is very effective in countering projectiles at ranges of 4-70 kms. Israel states that over 15,000 projectiles have been fired at population centres within the country, since 2000. The Iron Dome system had an interception rate of over 85 per cent, of projectiles deemed to be landing over populated centres. During the 2014 military confrontation Operation Protective Edge, for instance, out of the 4,500 rockets fired at Israel, at least 700 projectiles deemed as a threat by the system were intercepted, for an almost 85 per cent success rate.[6] During Operation Guardian of the Walls (2021), the system had a 90 per cent success rate, successfully taking out those determined as threatening population centres, out of the 4360 rockets fired from the Gaza Strip.[7]

As for defensive measures, Israel has built border perimeters across its land borders with its neighbouring countries, including Egypt, Syria, Jordan and ring-fenced the Palestinian territories in the Gaza Strip and the West Bank. Israel's borders with Egypt and Jordan are internationally recognized while the country's borders with Syria, Lebanon, West Bank and the Gaza Strip are not.

As with all its borders, security considerations play an important role in determining the country's border management policies. Israel's longest border, at 240 kms, is with Egypt, with which the country has a peace treaty dating back to 1979. The twin challenges that Israel has faced across its border with Egypt in recent times have been the terror threat from Sinai from radical Islamists as well as the problem of African refugees. The terror threat has significantly reduced, after the coming to power of the military government of Gen. Abdel Fatah Al-Sisi in 2013.

Israel's National Security Council (NSC) Counter-terrorism (CT) bureau reduced the threat level in southern Sinai to Israeli tourists from Level 1 (very high concrete threat) to Level 3 (basic concrete threat) in August 2021, the first time it did so in 17 years.[8] The threat level continues to remain high (Level 3) for areas in northern Sinai, while in the rest of Egypt for Israeli tourists, the categorization by the NSC is at Level 1.

The problem with the African refugees, primarily from conflict hotspots like Eritrea and Sudan, has significantly reduced due to a combination of executive and security steps that Israel has taken. These include strengthened border management policies, more robust border fencing, domestic executive measures that discourage employment opportunities for illegal migrants in tourist places like Eilat, for instance, and even paid schemes to deport refugees back to their home country or even other countries in Africa.

The Israel-West Bank barrier, meanwhile, has been touted as the largest construction project in Israeli history. The Second Intifada was a big catalyst for the barrier's construction, in order to prevent Palestinian suicide attacks. As noted in earlier sections, suicide attacks were responsible for nearly 40 per cent of all Israeli casualties since 2000. During the Second Intifada (2000-2007), 140 suicide attacks killed 542 Israeli citizens.[9] After the strengthened barrier, the number of suicide attacks drastically reduced, given that the next 14 years resulted in about 700 Israeli fatalities in total.

Palestinian terror groups, in fact, changed their tactics and increasingly resorted to launching crude rockets on Israeli population centres. Active defence measures like the Iron Dome have been very effective in countering such projectiles. While defensive perimeter solutions like security barriers have been very effective in countering terror threats, they have led to criticism relating to the movement of Palestinians, encroaching of Palestinian land and the charge of Israel being a 'walled state'. The following Table lists key Israeli kinetic and non-kinetic counter-terror measures in its fight against the Hezbollah and the Palestinian groups operating in the Gaza Strip.[10]

Israeli governments swear by the efficacy of the country's counter-terrorism strategy, given the drastic reduction in the fatalities of its citizens due to terrorist attacks, as well as due to the affirmed strength of the Israeli public (termed its 'resilience') to terrorist attacks. The Government's strong responses to incidents of terror or rocket strikes on its territory are touted as essential steps to restore deterrence. During the 2021 Gaza military action, taken in response to rocket strikes, Prime Minister Benjamin Netanyahu insisted that his government will 'take whatever action necessary to restore quiet and security to all residents of Israel'.[11] A few days earlier, Netanyahu asserted that Hamas 'will pay a very heavy price' for targeting Israeli population centres with missiles.[12]

Table 2: Israel's Kinetic and Non-Kinetic Responses to Terror Threats

Antagonist	*Nature of Response*	
	Kinetic	*Non-Kinetic*
Hezbollah	Military invasion and occupation (1982-2000)	Air raid shelters
	Large-scale use of air power (2006 Lebanon War);	Strengthening Home front command
	Targeted killings	Information warfare
	Air strikes against weapons depots, ammunition convoys, among others, not just on Lebanese territory but in places like Syria and even as far as Iraq	
	Active defence systems like 'David's Sling'	
Gaza Conflicts post-2005 Disengagement	Large-scale use of air-land forces;	Defensive perimeters with motion detection sensors, among other technological solutions;
	Targeted killings;	Economic warfare (land, air, and sea blockade; Tax revenues and electricity supply used as leverage)
	'Mowing the grass' tactics;	
	Wars of attrition;	
	Active defence systems like 'Iron Dome'	

Source: Author.

The large-scale air strikes, as well as land incursions into Gaza in the recent past, are viewed as imperative to degrade enemy capabilities. The Israeli tactics do result in significant loss of Palestinian lives and damage to infrastructure in the Gaza Strip. Israel, however, insists that the primary responsibility lies with the militant groups in the Gaza Strip using extremely congested civilian areas as launch pads to launch rocket and terror strikes in Israeli population areas.

India-Israel Internal Security/Counter-terror Cooperation

A significant amount of cooperation in the field of counter-terrorism and internal security has taken place between India and Israel, albeit, away from the public glare. As soon as full diplomatic relations were established, Indian leaders flagged counter-terrorism as a key area for cooperation. A month after India and Israel established full diplomatic ties, then Defence Minister Sharad Pawar identified this area as a key focus of cooperation,[13] and Ashok Tandon, the head of the National Security Guard (NSG), visited Israel as early as in 1995.

It is significant to point out that an Israeli delegation led by then National Security Adviser, Uzi Dayan, was on a visit to India, when Al Qaeda attacked New York on September 11, 2001. National Security Adviser Brajesh Mishra, addressing the American Jewish Committee's Annual Dinner in May 2003, a few months after 9/11, stated that India, the US and Israel have been 'prime targets of terrorism' and that all the three countries should jointly tackle the terror threat.[14]

The Joint Working Group on CT, however, was only established ten years after the establishment of full diplomatic ties, in 2002. Analysts opine that a possible reason for why counter-terrorism (CT) cooperation was not pursued vigorously till then, at least in the public domain, was because both countries faced different sources of threats.[15] Some analysts also flag 'domestic political sensitivity' for the apparent (public) lack of emphasis on CT cooperation.[16]

After the November 2008 Mumbai terror strikes, in which Israeli and Jewish citizens lost their lives, it could be argued that there was, in fact, greater congruence between the two countries in the arena of CT cooperation. India increasingly procured niche equipment to better equip its security forces to face the terror threat, even in places like Kashmir. Israeli assault weapons, for instance, became ubiquitous equipment for Indian security forces in such critical hotspots. Israel's Deputy Chief of General Staff, Maj. Gen. Moshe Kaplinsky had earlier in June 2007 visited Jammu and Kashmir, during his visit to India.[17]

Both countries signed an extradition treaty, during the visit of Foreign Minister S.M. Krishna in January 2012. The Foreign Minister's visit was to commemorate the 20th anniversary of the establishment of diplomatic ties. A homeland security (HLS) cooperation agreement was signed in February 2014, when P. Chidambaram was the Union Home Minister. Institutional interactions between the two countries relating to internal security have grown since then.

The joint steering committee on homeland security held its first meeting in September 2014. Four working groups, on border management, internal security, police modernization, capacity building and cyber-crime were established by this steering committee. Home Minister Rajnath Singh visited Israel in November 2014, when he was given a tour of the border areas with Yossi Cohen, the Israeli National Security Adviser. Since 2015, officer trainees of the National Police Academy, Hyderabad compulsorily visit the Israel National Police Academy for training.

After Singh's visit, Government sources indicated that India intends to get the benefit of Israel's border management expertise, as they are 'expert[s] in stopping infiltration by the use of advanced surveillance systems.' In the wake of the attacks on the Pathankot and Uri army bases in January and September 2016 respectively, analysts called for the Border Security Force (BSF) to use Israeli border guarding methods and solutions to better protect the borders.[18]

To be sure, India has been using Israeli equipment like the LORROS (Long-range Reconnaissance and Observation System) since at least 2008. Israeli UAVs have also been used extensively in areas like the Rann of Kutch. As noted earlier, senior Israeli officers also visited Kashmir. Maj. Gen. Kaplinsky visited Nagrota in 2007 while Israeli Army Chief Gen. Avi Mizrahi visited Akhnoor in September 2008.[19] The border guarding forces use high-tech surveillance devices, procured from Israel as well as manufactured domestically, to keep vigil on the border.

Minister of State in the Union Home Ministry, Kiren Rijuju informed the Rajya Sabha on March 2, 2016 that the Government would employ 'technological solutions in the form of integration of Radars, Sensors, Cameras, Communication Networks and Command and Control Solution along the Indo-Pakistan and the Indo-Bangladesh Border'.[20] Home Minister Rajnath Singh informed the Lok Sabha in August 2016 that the Government had decided to launch 'on a pilot basis' the Comprehensive Integrated Border Management System (CIBMS). The framework will include electro-optic sensors, radars, among other equipment, to complement human patrolling in areas of difficult terrain on the Indo-Pakistan border.[21]

Reports in May 2017 noted that India had procured high-technology border-fencing solutions from Israel. The head of the BSF, Director General K.K. Sharma affirmed in July 2018 that the technology and methods being used in the CIBMS were 'from Israel' and that the BSF border guarding philosophy would see a change in tactics from patrolling to quick reaction teams (QRT) and technological surveillance.[22] While the BSF ran limited pilot projects along the Indo-Pakistan and the Indo-Bangladesh border, it would seem, Israeli-style border solutions – with a heavy emphasis on sensors and high technology monitoring, coupled with minimal human interface, may not be smoothly integrated into the border security mechanisms.

To be sure, such technological solutions are critical in areas where round-the-clock human patrolling may not be feasible due to climatic or terrain conditions. There is also the issue of upkeep and maintenance of technological solutions, as well as proper training in order to deliver optimal results. Border guarding officials also emphasize that a one-size-fits-all approach may not be suitable for the border security requirements of a sub-continental-sized country like India.[23]

It is to be emphasized though, that technological solutions are being sought for an insignificant portion of the border. The Indo-Bangladesh border, for instance, is over 4,000 kms long, of which at least 75 per cent is fenced. Even out of the remaining 25 per cent of the border which is not fenced, guarding the border using the sole use of technology will be limited to a miniscule proportion of the border. Minister of State in the Union Home Ministry, Nityanand Rai, informed Parliament in November 2019 that just about 60 km out of the 400 km unfenced India-Bangladesh border 'will be covered by technological solutions'.[24] The unfenced areas are being monitored through human patrolling with the use of sophisticated equipment like hand-held thermal imagers, night vision devices, UAVs and LORROS, among others, some of which are procured from Israel.[25]

NOTES

1. Israel Tal, *National Security: The Israeli Experience* (Translated by Martin Kett), Praeger, London, 2000, p. 43.
2. Edward E. Azar, Paul Jureidini and Ronald McLaurin, 'Protracted Social Conflict: Theory and Practice in the Middle East', *Journal of Palestine Studies*, 8 (1), Autumn 1978, pp. 41-60, at https://www.jstor.org/stable/2536101 (Accessed February 15, 2022).
3. Efraim Inbar, *Israel's National Security: Issues and Challenges since the Yom Kippur War*, Routledge, London, 2008, p. 39.
4. Ministry of Foreign Affairs, 'In Memory of the Victims of Palestinian Violence and Terrorism in Israel', at https://mfa.gov.il/MFA/ForeignPolicy/Terrorism/Victims/Pages/In%20Memory%20of%20the%20Victims%20of%20Palestinian%20Violence%20a.aspx (Accessed February 15, 2022).
5. See Efraim Inbar and Eitan Shamir, 'Mowing the Grass: Israel's Strategy for Protracted Intractable Conflict', *Journal of Strategic Studies*, 37(1), 2014.
6. Israel Defense Force, 'Operation Protective Edge', August 26, 2014, at https://www.idf.il/en/minisites/wars-and-operations/operation-protective-edge/ (August 30, 2021).
7. Ministry of Foreign Affairs, 'Operation Guardian of the Walls', May 20, 2021, at https://www.gov.il/en/Departments/General/operation-guardian-of-the-walls-10-may-2021 (Accessed May 25, 2021).
8. The threat level was pegged at the highest in the aftermath of terror attacks targeting Israeli tourists in the southern Sinai beach resorts in 2004. See Israel National Security Council, 'Travel warnings', at https://www.nsc.gov.il/English/Travel-Warnings/Pages/allwarnings.aspx?l country=E (Accessed September 20, 2021).
9. Ministry of Foreign Affairs, 'Suicide and Other Bombing Attacks in Israel since the Declaration of Principles (September 1993),' Ministry of Foreign Affairs, April 19, 2016 (Updated), at https://www.mfa.gov.il/MFA/ForeignPolicy/Terrorism/Palestinian/Pages/Suicide%20and%20Other%20Bombing%20Attacks%20in%20Israel%20Since.aspx (Accessed September 5 2021).
10. See S. Samuel C. Rajiv, 'Israel and Hybrid Warfare', in Vikrant Deshpande (ed.), *Hybrid Warfare: The Changing Character of Conflict,* Pentagon Press, New Delhi, 2018, pp. 122-140.
11. Ministry of Foreign Affairs, 'Statement by PM Netanyahu', Ministry of Foreign Affairs, May 17, 2021, at https://mfa.gov.il/MFA/PressRoom/2021/Pages/Statement-by-PM-Netanyahu-17-May-2021.aspx (Accessed September 5, 2021).
12. Ministry of Foreign Affairs, 'Statement by PM Netanyahu following a security assessment at the Kirya', Ministry of Foreign Affairs, May 14, 2021, at https://mfa.gov.il/MFA/PressRoom/

2021/Pages/Statement-by-PM-Netanyahu-14-Mayb2021.aspx (Accessed September 5, 2021).

13. P.R. Kumaraswamy, 'India and Israel: Evolving Strategic Partnership', Begin-Sadat Center for Strategic Studies, 1998, p. 11at http://www.jstor.com/stable/resrep04726.6 (Accessed September 5, 2021).
14. Ministry of External Affairs, 'Address by Shri Brajesh Mishra, National Security Adviser at the American Jewish Committee Annual Dinner', Ministry of External Affairs, May 8, 2003, at https://www.mea.gov.in/Speeches-Statements.htm?dtl/4526/Address+by+Shri+Brajesh+Mishra+National+Security+Advisor+at+the+American+Jewish+Committee+Annual+Dinner (Accessed September 5, 2021).
15. See Rajendra Abhyankar, 'The Evolution and Future of India-Israel Relations', Research Paper No. 6, 2012, p. 20, S. Daniel Abraham Centre for International and Regional Studies, at http://www.tau.ac.il/humanities/abraham/india-israel.pdf (Accessed December 26, 2015); See also, Efraim Inbar, 'The India-Israeli Entente', p. 93; Kumaraswamy, 'India and Israel: Emerging Partnership', no. 152, p. 202.
16. Monika Chansoria in 'Countering Terrorism through International Cooperation' in Gurmeet Kanwal and N. Manoharan (eds.), *India's War on Terror,* Knowledge World, New Delhi, 2010, pp. 189-190.
17. Cherian Samuel, 'India, Israel and the US Factor', in Eytan Gilboa and Efraim Inbar (eds.), *US-Israeli Relations in a New Era,* Routledge, 2009, p. 199; Rajat Pandit, 'Israeli Army team to visit J&K', *The Times of India*, June 8, 2007, at https://timesofindia.indiatimes.com/india/Fighting-terror-Israeli-army-team-to-visit-JK/articleshow/2107689.cms (Accessed September 5, 2021).
18. Aman Sharma, 'Pathankot attack: Follow Israel's top-notch technology tricks to protect India-Pakistan border', *The Economic Times*, July 10, 2018, at https://economictimes.indiatimes.com/news/defence/pathankot-attack-follow-israels-top-notch-technology-tricks-to-protect-india-pakistan-border/articleshow/50598420.cms (Accessed September 5, 2021).
19. Yaakov Katz, 'India seeks IDF help in Kashmir conflict', *The Jerusalem Post*, September 14, 2008, at https://www.jpost.com/international/india-seeks-idf-help-in-kashmir-conflict (Accessed September 5, 2021).
20. Rajya Sabha, 'Gaps in security framework on international border in Punjab', Unstarred Question No. 703, March 2, 2016, at https://rajyasabha.nic.in/rsnew/Questions/QResult.aspx (Accessed September 5, 2021).
21. Lok Sabha, 'Border management', Starred Question No. 326, August 9, 2016, at http://loksabhaph.nic.in/Questions/QResult15.aspx?qref=39445&lsno=16 (Accessed September 5, 2021).
22. Press Trust of India, 'Israel fence systems, quick response team at Pakistan borders: BSF DG', July 13, 2018, at https://economictimes.indiatimes.com/news/defence/israel-fence-systems-quick-response-team-at-pakistan-borders-bsf-dg/articleshow/60044263.cms?from=mdr (Accessed September 5, 2021).
23. Interactions with officials of the Border Security Force (BSF), at training programmes conducted by MP-IDSA, New Delhi.
24. Lok Sabha, 'Border fencing', Unstarred Question No. 458, November 19, 2019, at http://loksabhaph.nic.in/Questions/QResult15.aspx?qref=6699&lsno=17 (Accessed September 5, 2021).
25. Lok Sabha, 'Border fencing', Unstarred Question No. 2308, August 3, 2021, at http://loksabhaph.nic.in/Questions/QResult15.aspx?qref=26717&lsno=17 (Accessed September 5, 2021).

4

HIGH-TECHNOLOGY COOPERATION

India and Israel have established long-standing and significant cooperation in the field of science and technology, spanning the innovation, agriculture, water and the space sectors. The following sections will briefly highlight pertinent aspects of cooperation in these varied fields, with both sides having ambitious plans to ramp up their strategic partnership in these sectors.

Innovation Sector Cooperation

India-Israel science and technology cooperation dates back to the May 1993 agreement between the two countries on the issue, which was the second agreement that the two countries signed after the 1992 agreement normalizing relations. This indicates the focus and priority given to this aspect of bilateral cooperation, very early on at the start of their diplomatic journey. In December of that same year, India and Israel kick-started their cooperation in the agriculture sector, which has since become one of the most visible mainstays of their bilateral scientific engagement.

Cooperation in the innovation sector takes place under the rubric of the Department of Science and Technology (DST), Government of India and the Israel Innovation Authority (IIA) of the Government of Israel. While the Indian implementing agency is the Global Innovation and Technology Alliance (GITA), the Israel implementing agency is the Israeli Industry Center for

Research and Development. GITA is a unique public-private partnership (PPP) with joint funding by the Confederation of Indian Industry (CII) and the Technology Development Board (TDB) of the DST. GITA is involved in bilateral R&D projects with many countries, including Canada, Finland, Italy, Republic of Korea, Spain, Sweden, and the United Kingdom, apart from Israel. Israel is an essential partner in national developmental missions of the Government of India, like Swacch Bharat, Make In India, Digital India and National Mission for Sustainable Agriculture.[1]

In March 2010, a Working Programme was signed between India and Israel for establishing science and technology cooperation and to extend financial support for joint R&D activities. An allocation of Rs 4 crores to support 10 projects for a period of two years was made.[2] During the path-breaking visit of Prime Minister Modi to Israel in July 2017, a Memorandum of Understanding was signed, as part of which both countries created the $40 million India-Israel Industrial R&D and Technological Innovation Fund (I4F Fund), with equal contributions of $4 million over a period of five years. The programme provides funds to Indian and Israeli researchers to engage in cutting-edge joint research in innovative areas. These areas relate to agriculture, energy, healthcare, information and communication technologies (ICT) and water. The first call for joint R&D proposals was issued in January 2018, when Prime Minister Netanyahu visited India. Subsequent call for proposals were issued in August 2018, January 2019, August 2019, January 2020, August 2020, January 2021, September 2021 and March 2022. Till mid-2021, 15 joint projects had been awarded, related to cutting-edge issues in agriculture, irrigation, the telecom sector and medical diagnostics, among others.[3]

Cooperation with Israel, the 'Start-Up' nation, has indeed picked up in recent times. As per the Global Innovation Index 2022, which ranks over 130 countries based on more than 80 indicators, Israel was the most innovative economy in the West Asia and North Africa (WANA) region, followed by the United Arab Emirates (UAE) and Turkiye. Overall, Israel was ranked as the 16th most innovative country in the world, in the list topped by Switzerland. In 2019, Israel was among the top 10 innovative economies in the world. Among the areas that Israel has a lead include those relating to markets and business sophistication (on aspects like ease of getting credit, FDI net inflows, and university-industry collaboration), human capital, knowledge and technology outputs (expenditure on education, tertiary education enrolment, patents and high-technology exports).[4]

In terms of research and development (R&D) expenditure, Israel occupied the first position globally, spending 5.4 per cent of its GDP on R&D activities.[5] In comparison, the Organisation for Economic Cooperation and Development (OECD) countries spend less than half of what Israel spends as a percentage of GDP on R&D expenditure.[6] Over 11 per cent of Israel's total trade is made up of high-tech exports, while information, communications and technology (ICT) exports make up over 15 per cent of its total trade. Israel has the highest per capita number of R&D centres of multi-national corporations (MNC) on its soil.[7]

India, meanwhile, was placed at the 40th position in the 2022 Index—the third time it broke into the Top 50 rankings, after its 48th position in 2020 and 46th position in 2021. In 2019, India was placed at the 62nd position. India was the most innovative country in Central and Southern Asia, followed by Iran. India, along with China, the United States, United Kingdom and Germany, was, among the top five countries for scientific output, as per the 2021 Index.[8] India's ICT exports make up 14 per cent of its total trade, as per the 2022 report, while high-tech exports are at 4.4 per cent of its total trade. India spends just 0.7 per cent of its GDP on R&D, and holds the 53rd rank globally.[9] Analysts note that private sector investment in the R&D sector is particularly limited in India, while all over the world, the private sector plays a significant role in fostering innovation.[10]

When Prime Minister Netanyahu visited India in January 2018, he visited the innovation hub, iCreate Centre in Ahmedabad, along with Prime Minister Modi and inaugurated the International Centre for Entrepreneurship and Technology. The hub was established by the Gujarat government as a technology and start-up incubator. A MoU was signed with the Israel Institute of Technology (IIT), Technion in 2012 to jointly incubate Start-Ups. Students from Gujarat universities, including the Indian Institute of Technology (IIT) Gandhinagar, visit Technion every year to experience the country's innovation eco-system.

Israel has also opened a Consulate in the hi-tech city, Bengaluru, in 2013.

At the time of the opening of the Consulate, Israeli officials noted that it was important for their country to have a presence in the technology capital of India. Karnataka is also perhaps the only state in India which has signed a R&D MoU with Israel—the Karnataka Israel Industrial Research and Development Programme (KIIRD). The agreement, signed in 2013, seeks to support joint R&D projects between the state and Israeli researchers. The programme supports projects in the areas of bio-informatics, green technologies, nanotechnology, among others, which can be adopted for use by the state.

While the Israel Innovation Authority is the funding and implementing agency from the Israeli side, the Karnataka State Council for Science and Technology is the implementing Agency and Karnataka Science and Technology Promotion Agency in the funding agency for the state government. Some of the programmes that have been carried out as part of the KIIRD project include those relating to innovative devices for treatment of female urinary continence and titanium hoses for aerospace applications.[11] While the medical device project was funded to the tune of Rs 90 lakhs, the titanium hoses project was funded to the tune of Rs 2.5 crore.[12]

Israel's innovation cooperation with not just India but with other countries is indeed significant. The Israel Industry Center for Research and Development (known by its Hebrew acronym, Matimop) has bilateral federal cooperation programmes with over 25 countries and also with over 20 state governments and municipalities in these countries, separately. As noted above, in the case of India, at the federal level, the I4RD is the framework for cooperation in the innovation sector while at state governmental level, the KIRD programme is a pertinent example. At the level of the civil society also, initiatives like the India-Israel Innovation Centre were launched in Bengaluru in October 2018.

Israel's Cooperation with Other Countries in Innovation Sphere

Israel has bilateral R&D cooperation programmes with countries as varied as Uruguay to Australia, Argentina, the European Union, Japan, Taiwan, among others. The innovation sector cooperation with the United States is governed by the Binational Industrial Research and Development (BIRD) Foundation, established in 1977. The programme has funded over 1000 projects since inception and the total sales of products developed through the programmes exceeds $10 billion. Over 30 projects are awarded each year currently, with two specific funding cycles pertaining to energy and homeland security.[13] In 2020, for instance, maximum number of projects were on issues relating to energy, water and environment, followed by life sciences. A unique addition to the BIRD framework is the Trilateral Industrial Development (TRIDE) Fund, managed by Israel, the US and Jordan. This fund was established in 1996, two years after the establishment of full diplomatic relations between Israel and Jordan through their 1994 peace treaty.

Perhaps the most significant cooperation in the innovation sphere Israel has currently, apart from the US and the EU countries, is with the People's Republic of China. Both countries entered into a 'Comprehensive Innovation Partnership' agreement in 2017, during the visit of Prime Minister Netanyahu. Prior to Netanyahu's visit, the China-Israel Innovation Development Fund was founded in 2014 and a three-year action plan on innovation cooperation was signed in 2015, co-terminus with the establishment of the China-Israel Joint Committee on Innovation Cooperation.

In 2018, China-Israel bilateral trade was almost $14 billion, as against $10 billion in 2011. Multiple rounds of negotiations have been conducted on a free trade agreement (FTA) since 2015 and both sides hope to conclude an agreement before the end of 2022. The Israel Innovation Authority's 'Innovation in Israel 2016' report pegged the value of Chinese investments in Israeli companies at $500 million. A 2020 RAND study states that total Chinese investments in Israel at close to $12 billion.[14]

Israeli agencies have city-specific MoUs with Chinese cities like Shanghai and Shenzhen. Both the Shenzhen and the Shanghai-Israel Programme for Industrial R&D dates back to 2011. The first joint call for projects as part of the China Ministry of Science and Technology (MOST)-Israel joint R&D programme was issued in May 2012. As per the Chinese Ministry of Commerce (MOFCOM), China has 17 offshore centres of innovation established in Israel.[15]

Chinese government-backed companies have also won huge infrastructure projects in Israel, and are currently running three out of the four ports in the country—Haifa, Ashdod and Eilat. Israel is under pressure from the US regarding the security implications of Chinese companies running the sensitive Haifa port, for instance. US administrations, beginning from Donald Trump to Joe Biden, have highlighted these concerns regarding such projects.[16] Reports in February 2021 noted that Israel rejected a US Coast Guard request to inspect the Haifa port, being run by the Shanghai International Port Group (SIPG). Analysts note that the sensitivities for the US are on account of the fact that the port operations centre is near Israel's main naval base and the SIPG will be in charge of the internet systems for port operations, which could be used for information manipulation or data mining.[17] The SIPG began operations at the Haifa port in September 2021 and will be in charge of the port for 25 years.

In order to better regulate Chinese investments in Israel, the Israeli government created the Advisory Committee to Inspect National Security Aspects of Foreign Investments, on the lines of the US Committee on Foreign Investment in the United States (CFIUS) in October 2019. This committee began functioning from January 2020.[18] Analysts though note that the Committee was created through a Cabinet decision and is not legislatively-mandated and hence, is susceptible to government pressure to modulate its decisions.[19]

Chinese investments in Israeli high-tech companies and Start-Ups create a unique complication for Israel. At one level, these investments and exposure allow the Chinese access to cutting-edge Israeli research and products in niche areas like robotics, among others. Israel is one of the world's leaders in the export of unmanned aerial vehicles (UAVs) also. China has emerged as a big player in the UAV export market in recent years, with significant customers in West Asian states. The Israel Innovation Report 2016 alludes to this fact when it notes that growing Chinese (as well as American) presence in the international UAV market 'threatens Israeli leadership in the field of military robotics'.[20] The 2018-19 report of the Israel Innovation Authority, meanwhile, also highlighted China's efforts to be a world leader in artificial technologies (AI) by 2030 and its investments in this sector, totaling tens of billions of dollars.[21]

Even as Israel grapples with the implications of Chinese challenge in the high-tech sphere, domestically, the innovation landscape in Israel is witnessing a change. The Israel Innovation Authority draws attention to what it terms as the 'maturing' of the Israeli high-tech sector, with more companies getting listed on the stock exchanges, the need for regulatory and funding mechanisms to keep pace with the requirements of such companies—to undertake activities such as mergers and acquisitions, among others. The latest report of the IIA also flags concerns over the limited governmental support for R&D funding in the country—with the private sector overwhelmingly funding such activities.[22]

Prospects

In the above context of the ongoing India-Israel bilateral cooperation—with programmes like the I4F proceeding apace, Israel's on-going cooperation with other countries—specifically China in the innovation sphere, coupled with the wariness of the US about the growing Chinese presence and stakes in Israel's economy, there is even greater space for expanding the scope of cooperation between India and Israel, bilaterally as well as in conjunction with other countries, in the innovation sphere. India, for instance, has become the world's third largest start-up ecosystem in the world.

The first-ever Start-up India Innovation Week was organized in January 2022 by the Department for the Promotion of Industry and Internal Trade (DPIIT), to showcase the breadth of entrepreneurship across India, where the winners of the National Start-Up Awards 2021 were announced. DPIIT Secretary Anurag Jain noted that over 60,000 start-ups have been recognized by his Ministry till date and that over 40 Unicorns (companies with valuation of over $1 billion) were added in the year 2021 itself, equal to the number of unicorns created over the past nine years cumulatively.[23] Over 600,000 jobs have been created since 2016 by these start-ups.

As per the India Innovation Index 2020, among Indian states, Karnataka occupies the top position as the most innovative state in the country, followed by Maharashtra, Tamil Nadu, Telangana, Kerala, Haryana, Andhra Pradesh, Gujarat, Uttar Pradesh and Punjab.[24] As noted earlier, Karnataka is the only state government with which Israel has an on-going programme in the innovation sphere. Other states can take a leaf out of the Karnataka handbook and perhaps earmark specific budgets for joint funding R&D programmes with Israeli government agencies and/or private entities. It is pertinent to note that this kind of cooperation exists on a large scale with many US states, even as at the federal level, programmes like the BIRD Foundation have been in existence for over six decades.

The government has placed a premium on innovation-led economic growth, to make the country a $5 trillion economy in the near future. The Office of the Principal Scientific Advisor's draft 'Science, Technology and Innovation Policy 2020' document lays out an ambitious agenda to create and nurture a cutting-edge innovation eco-system in the country. Among other initiatives, it envisages the creation of a Strategic Technology Board/ Fund to promote technological self-reliance and indigenization, fostering science and technology-led entrepreneurship, increase in R&D spending, and the creation of a national repository for science, technology, innovation (STI). The document calls for the creation of international knowledge centres to promote global knowledge and talent exchange.

At the international level, the aim is to assume a more pro-active role for agenda-setting in the global science and technology discourse, relating to regulations and standards concerning futuristic and dual-use technologies. It calls for customized science and technology engagement strategies at the bilateral/multi-lateral/regional levels and for mission-oriented approach aligned with foreign policy priorities.[25] The policy document, therefore, gels well with the importance of further enhancing the scope and range of the India-Israel innovation cooperation.

India and Israel, on their part, can further expand science and technology partnership, not just bilaterally at the federal and state levels, but also tri-laterally (with countries like the United States) and at the quadrilateral level (with countries like the UAE). India-US science and technology cooperation, for instance, has many facets, including frameworks like the India-US S&T Forum (IUSSTF)—established in 2000, the India-US S&T Endowment Fund (IUSSTEF)—set up in 2009, among others. The Fund provides project support to the tune of approximately $400,000 (Rs 2.5 crore) for joint projects in areas like agriculture, education, water, financial inclusion, diagnostic devices, among others. One of its recent initiatives is the Covid-19 Ignition Grants to eleven bilateral teams launched in April 2020, which had proposed innovative ideas to counter the pandemic. These grants related to diagnostics monitoring, public health and safety, communication aspects, among others.[26]

Significant activities as part of the IUUSTF include exchange programmes with top US engineering and scientific institutions, as well as programmes supported by the industry on areas like genome engineering, water research, clean energy, solar research, among others.[27] Over 400 workshops have been held as part of the IUSSTF's activities in the past two decades, on areas relating to life, chemical, engineering, physical, as well as earth and atmospheric sciences. During 2015-20, nearly half of these workshops related to the life and medical sciences field. India's Science and Research Engineering Board (SERB) also supports proposals that compete for funding from the US National Science Foundation's (NSF) Partnerships for International Research and Education (PIRE).

The most significant bilateral cooperation for Israel in the S&T field, as noted in earlier sections, is with the US, through the BIRD mechanism. Lawmakers in the US Congress have been at the forefront, recommending trilateral cooperation between India, Israel and US in the fields of innovation as well as national security. An amendment, for instance, was inserted in the Intelligence Authorisation Act 2016, by US Congressmen Joe Crowley, Eliot Engel, Ami Bera, among others, calling for a report from the Director of National Intelligence (DNI) on the possibilities of increasing national security cooperation between the three countries.[28] Way back in May 2003, as noted in Chapter Three, National Security Advisor Brajesh Misra had pointed out that India, Israel and the US were victims of terrorism and called for joint efforts on the part of the three countries to counter the problem. Interestingly, the address was in the aftermath of the 9/11 attacks, at an event organized by the American Jewish Committee.

Analysts have also called for developing an India-Israel-US defence innovation partnership to leverage each other's strengths and exploit the potential of futuristic technologies for mutual benefit, specifically among the defence innovation organisations of the three countries.[29] All three governments actively support start-ups, which aim to manufacture cutting-edge products in the national security sphere.[30] In India, the iDEX programme has funded

Start-Ups like Tonbo Imaging, for instance, which now has an increasingly global clientele.

The contours are emerging of quadrilateral cooperation between India, Israel, the UAE and Israel. During the visit of Foreign Minister Jaishankar to Israel in October 2021, the first ever (virtual) meeting between the Foreign Ministers of the four countries took place, wherein, all sides agreed to launch a joint economic forum. Then Israeli Foreign Minister Yair Lapid was quoted as stating that the four sides will explore opportunities in joint infrastructure projects, among others.[31] An Israeli company, Eccopia, signed the first trilateral joint venture in May 2021, as part of which it would produce robotic solar cleaning technology in factories in India, for eventual use in the UAE.[32] The International Federation of Indo-Israel Chambers of Commerce, at the launch of which this trilateral project was announced, with headquarters in Dubai, has projected that the volume of business between the three countries could cross $110 billion by 2030.

There has been a massive increase in the volume and scope of interactions between the UAE and Israel in the aftermath of the Abraham Accords. The volume of bilateral trade, for instance, has already crossed $500 million. Prime Minister Naftali Bennet travelled to Abu Dhabi in December 2021, for the first such visit by an Israeli prime minister. Prime Minister Netanyahu, under whose leadership the Abraham Accords were launched, could not formally visit the UAE.

Israel-UAE relations also survived Israel's military operations in the Gaza Strip—Operation Guardian of the Walls, in May 2021. Nearly 4500 rockets were fired from the Gaza Strip towards Israeli population centres. The Iron Dome missile defence system successfully intercepted nearly 90 per cent of rockets whose trajectory was deemed by the system to be falling in civilian areas. The Israel Defense Force (IDF) responded by striking nearly 1500 targets inside the Palestinian territories and took out many Palestinians, who were heading militant organizations in the territory.[33]

Israel's military operations inside the Gaza Strip—in the aftermath of the 2005 Gaza disengagement by the Ariel Sharon government, have resulted in the significant loss of Palestinian lives. Israel insists it needs to undertake such operations periodically to maintain deterrence and prevent economic disruption and loss of lives of Israeli citizens. The fact that Israel-UAE relations did not get much affected by the latest Israeli military action, to many Israeli analysts, was proof that the Palestinian issue did not occupy the same level of interest and concern as in the past. The UAE, for instance, did not take steps like recalling its Ambassador from Tel Aviv during the conflict.[34] The Israeli government, on its part, contends that they are only responding to rocket attacks from the Palestinian groups and that it has every right to pursue measures for self-defence.

Given the above reality of continued Israel-UAE bonhomie irrespective of the developments relating to the Palestinian issue, and growing Israel-UAE economic interactions, the stage is set for enhancing trilateral cooperation with India, who is a strategic partner for both countries. The UAE in March 2021 announced the setting up of a $10 billion investment fund for investments specifically focused on Israeli companies and start-ups working on such issues as energy, water, agri-tech, space and healthcare.[35] The fund made its first investment of $100 million in January 2022 in an Israeli technology firm.

India-UAE relations, meanwhile are robust and are gaining new strength. Bilateral trade in 2021-22 stood at nearly $73 billion. Pre-Covid, in 2019-20, the total volume of bilateral trade was nearly $60 billion. India and the UAE signed the Comprehensive Economic Partnership Agreement (CEPA) in February 2022. Both the countries have an ambitious agenda to expand the volume of bilateral trade (in goods) to $100 billion and trade in services to over $15 billion within the next five years.

India, Israel and the US are also collaborating in 5G technology, as per the Deputy Administrator for the US Agency for International Development (USAID), Bonnie Glick.[36] In June 2020, Senators Mark Warner and John Cornyn moved an amendment to the National Defence Authorisation Act 2021 calling for an assessment from Defence Secretary Mark Esper on whether the BIRD Foundation provides a model for US-India private sector collaboration on defence technologies.[37] Both the Senators are Chairmen of the Senate India Caucus. As noted in earlier sections, the US and Israel have indeed expanded the scope of operations of the binational BIRD Foundation to include Jordan as part of the TRIDE Fund, established in 1996. This fund was mostly related to R&D activities in the civil society sphere.

While Defence Secretary Esper's assessment is not in the public domain, the Senator's specific query was whether the BIRD model could assist in the development of defence technologies in the India-US context, specifically as it relates to the private sector. It is pertinent to point out that the BIRD Foundation grants are not related to Israel-US defence technology development, an area covered by their 10-year defence cooperation agreement. The current agreement, valid from 2019-2028, provides Israel with $3.3 billion annually in foreign military financing (FMF) and $500 million in missile defence cooperative programmes. Israel is the largest recipient of US security assistance under the FMF programme.[38] The India-US Defence Technology and Trade Initiative (DTTI), meanwhile, governs aspects relating to co-production and co-development of defence technologies. As part of the DTTI, four working groups relating to land, naval, air and aircraft carrier technology are in operation. The first project as part of the DTTI was signed in September 2020, relating to the co-development of an air launched unmanned aerial vehicle (UAV).[39]

The first meeting of the I2U2—dubbed the 'West Asian Quad', meanwhile, took place in July 2022, during President Biden's visit to Israel. Prime Minister Modi and UAE President Sheikh Mohammed Bin Zayed Al Nahyan participated virtually in the Summit. The Summit grew out of the October 2021 meeting between the foreign ministers of the four countries, which incidentally happened when External Affairs Minister S. Jaishankar was visiting Israel.

The MEA in a statement, ahead of the Summit, noted that the grouping will focus on cooperation on six areas—water, energy, transportation, space, health and food security.[40] A key outcome of the summit was the decision to establish integrated food parks across India, with $2 billion of UAE investment. The group will also establish a 300 MW wind and solar plant in Gujarat, worth $330 million, a feasibility study for which was funded by the US Trade and Development Agency.

The new mini-lateral is a major development that brings together these four countries with a common geo-economic vision pertaining to enhancing the well-being of their peoples, shunning long-held ideological binaries that prevented mutually beneficial cooperation. The Abraham Accords of August 2020 and the Modi government's robust bilateral engagement with key stakeholders in the region, have led to the creation of what promises to be a key instrument furthering regional strategic stability and mutual economic prosperity.

Agriculture Sector Cooperation

India-Israel cooperation in the agriculture sector dates back to the December 1993 Memorandum of Understanding (MoU) in this field, which was further strengthened by the December 1996 Memorandum of Intent on Joint High-Tech Agricultural Demonstration Project. An Executive Agreement for a Programme of Cooperation in the agriculture sector was signed in October 1997. The Three-Year Work Plan for Cooperation in the Agriculture Sector, meanwhile, was signed in May 2006. The agreement for the second and the third phases was signed in May 2011 and January 2015 respectively. The agreement for the fourth phase of cooperation for three years was signed during the visit to Israel of Prime Minister Modi in July 2017.

MASHAV, the Israel Agency for International Development Cooperation, is the overall agency for cooperation in this sector, while CINADCO, the Center for International Agriculture Development Cooperation, which is part of the Israeli Ministry of Agriculture, is the professional agency responsible for implementation of the country's agriculture programmes with India. The National Horticulture Mission at the Agriculture Ministry—also termed the Mission for Integrated Development of Horticulture (MIDH), is the nodal agency on the Indian side. MASHAV also has a MoU with the International Crops Research Institute for the Semi-Arid Tropics (ICRISAT), located outside Hyderabad, signed in February 2007. The principal aim of this agreement is to share know-how and technology and strengthen the capabilities of national agricultural research institutions.

It is pertinent to note that in December 2007, the United Nations General Assembly (UNGA) adopted a resolution initiated by Israel on 'Agricultural Technology for Development'. This was the first resolution adopted by the UN on an Israeli-sponsored resolution. The resolution reaffirms the aspirations of the Millennium Development Goals (MDG) to reduce world poverty and hunger by half by 2015 and urges developed nations to share agricultural knowledge and technologies with developing countries in a fair and transparent manner.[41] MASHAV's more than 50 years of experience in assisting developing countries in developmental projects guided the Israeli Foreign Ministry's action in initiating this resolution.

The first India-Israel Agriculture Project (IIAP), meanwhile, began in 2008 and has since been extended for subsequent three-year intervals, in 2011, 2015, 2017 and 2021 respectively. Nearly Rs. 254 crores have been spent on the IIAP since inception, in 14 states of India, across four phases, till 2021, with the maximum amount spent in Haryana, with projects being implemented in the state in all four phases.

Table 3: India-Israel Agricultural Project: State Projects and Amount Spent

S. No.	*States*	*Amount Spent (in lakhs)*	*Projects Implemented in Phases*
1	Haryana	5143.35	Phases 1-IV
2	Punjab	3508	Phase II
3	Maharashtra	2292	Phase 1
4	Gujarat	1997.5	Phase II
5	Tamil Nadu	1898	Phase II
6	Madhya Pradesh	1637.49	Phase IV
7	Bihar	1570	Phase II
8	Uttar Pradesh	1520	Phase II
9	Rajasthan	1491	Phase II
10	Karnataka	1024.03	Phase II
11	Telangana	920	Phase II
12	Mizoram	900	Phase III
13	Andhra Pradesh	892	Phase III
14	Assam	583.58	Phase IV
Total		25376.95	

Source: Adapted from Press Information Bureau, 'Status of Centres of Excellence under Indo-Israel Cooperation', at https://static.pib.gov.in/WriteReadData/specificdocs/documents/2021/may/doc202152421.pdf (Accessed October 5, 2021).

During the visit of Prime Minister Modi to Israel in July 2017, the agriculture plan was extended till 2021. Most recently, in May 2021, the fifth India-Israel Agriculture Project (IIAP) Work Plan was agreed upon, valid till 2023. Areas in which Israeli expertise is being imparted include water and soil management, arid and semi-arid crop production, food and vegetable production, plant protection and control, farm mechanization, agriculture training to Indian farmers, post-harvest management, water resource management, animal husbandry and dairying, among other significant steps. At least 25 million high quality vegetable seedlings are produced by these centres, apart from imparting training to over 100,000 farmers in latest technology in horticulture.[42]

Centres of Excellence (CoE) in agriculture have been established to demonstrate technologies and impart training. The Gharaunda CoE in Karnal, Haryana was the first such centre to be set up under the project. As of December 2021, as many as 30 such centres are operating in ten states of India, including in Bihar, Gujarat, Karnataka, Maharashtra, Punjab, Rajasthan, Tamil Nadu, Uttar Pradesh, and West Bengal.[43] These centres relate to crops, fruits and vegetables as varied as citrus, mango, pomegranate, dates and banana-palm, apart from activities like bee-keeping. A MoU for CoE in Animal Husbandry and Dairy Farming was signed in April 2015, which was set up in Hisar, Haryana. A model dairy farm was established to show-case beneficial technologies at the State Cattle Breeding Project at Hisar. Programmes to help in the genetic improvement of local herds through imported germplasm were also being implemented.[44]

Going forward, as part of the agriculture Work Plan, both sides intend to establish 'Indo-Israel Villages of Excellence' (IIVOE) to develop a model eco-system of farming best practices. Initially, this project is expected to be started around 13 CoE's and will involve at least 75 villages nearby these Centres, in eight states.[45] The specific focus of this programme is to help in the building of modern agriculture infrastructure, capacity building and help establish market linkages.

Water Sector Cooperation

Cooperation in the water sector received high attention during the visit of Prime Minister Modi to Israel in July 2017. India and Israel signed a 'Strategic Partnership in Water and Agriculture' during that historic visit, apart from acknowledging the 'Strategic Partnership' framework for the overall relationship. Out of the seven MoUs that were signed during that visit, two of them related to cooperation in this sector. These included a MoU on water utility reform in Uttar Pradesh and the national water conservation mission of the Ministry of Drinking Water and Sanitation. About seven months prior to the visit of Modi, in November 2016, another MoU was signed by the Ministry of Water Resources, River Development and Ganga Rejuvenation to make use of Israel's expertise in water rejuvenation, waste water recycling and re-use, water conservation and water resource management.

Israel is one among 14 countries with which the Ministry of Water Resources has signed an agreement in the field of water management. The Ministry has a Joint Working Group (JWG) to implement the mandate and activities of the MoU. A Centre of Excellence for treatment of Brackish Water has also been set up in Bathinda, Punjab. The original agreement with Israel on water sector cooperation dates back to December 1993, when the Ministry of Agriculture signed an agreement with their Israeli counterparts for cooperation in the fields of water and soil management.[46]

During the visit of President Rueven Rivlin in November 2016, a MoU on Water Resources Management and Development Cooperation was signed to seek Israeli expertise in addressing the issue of water shortages in India, given its established track record in water management. Israel, despite being one of the world's most water-stressed countries, has mastered the art of water management and waste water recycling. Over 60 per cent of the country is desert and the Sea of Galilee is the only freshwater source for the country.

It is important to note that Israel was facing frequent droughts till the 1990s. The government swung into action and constituted a committee in 2002, which led to the establishment of the Israel Water Authority (IWA) in 2007, an autonomous agency with responsibilities for managing the water supply chain. The water supply eco-system is funded almost entirely by the user's tariffs and is efficiently run, with innovative technologies like water desalination plants, efficient irrigation systems, waste water re-use and recycling, use of water aquifers and interception of surface water run-offs, among others.[47] Over 50 per cent of Israel's water needs for agriculture purposes, for instance, are met by water desalination.[48] This, even as Israel has reduced the water required for irrigation purposes by the use of efficient techniques like drip irrigation, by at least 30 per cent.[49]

Israel's Ministry of Foreign Affairs notes that the country's dependence on renewable, fresh, natural water (RFNW) has witnessed a remarkable decrease, from over 500 cubic meters (cm) per year in the 1960s to less than 100 cm per year by 2015. This was achieved by increased use of such techniques like re-use and recycling of water as well as building of water desalination plants.[50] Israel currently generates nearly 55 per cent of its water requirements from water desalination. The Sorek desalination plant, near Tel Aviv, is the largest reverse osmosis facility in the world. Israeli analysts proudly note that their country is the only one in the dry Middle East that is not suffering an acute water shortage.[51] Water shortages, in fact, analysts note, was a key contributing factor that led to widespread unrest and fueled the mass uprising against the Assad government.[52]

In the transformed regional geo-politics post the Abraham Accords, Israel's neighbours like Jordan are taking advantage of the country's water prowess to address their pressing water shortages. Amman, the UAE and Israel signed a tri-partite agreement in November 2021, as part of which, an Emirati fund will finance a solar power plant in Jordan, which will supply 'green' electricity to Israel, which in turn, will supply desalinated water to its neighbour.[53] Reports note that currently, about 6 per cent of the country's desalinated water is piped to Jordan and the Palestinian territories.[54]

As for Israel's ongoing cooperation in the water sector with Indian state and federal governments, the Brihanmumbai Municipal Corporation (BMC) signed a Memorandum of Understanding (MoU) with the Israeli water desalination pioneer, IDE Technologies Limited, in June 2021 for preparation of a project report for 200 million liters per day (MLD) water desalination plant, which can be expanded to 400 MLD per day. The state's first water desalination plant for non-potable use is slated to become operational in 2025, at an expected cost of Rs 1600 crores.[55] Some concerns though have been raised over the possible negative environmental impact of desalination plants on Mumbai's coastline.[56]

The IDE was also involved in building the 100 million litres per day (MLD) Nemelli water desalination plant, off the coast of Chennai, in association with VA Tech Wabag and Larsen and Toubro. The work began in 2010 and the plant was commissioned in February 2013. The tenders for the construction of two more plants, a 150 MLD capacity one and a 400 MLD capacity one, have been awarded to Spanish and Australian firms. Both the plants are expected to be completed in 2022 and 2024 respectively.[57]

The Lok Sabha was informed in November 2016 that India and Israel had signed a MoU for cooperation in the fields of water resources management and development, with water desalination an important and essential part of collaboration. The Union Minister of State for Water Resources, Sanjeev Baliyan, informed the House that the government also planned to incentivize the use of desalination technologies to meet the country's growing water requirements.[58]

Gujarat is another Indian state intending to make use of the Israeli water desalination technology. Then Chief Minister Vijay Rupani visited Israel in June 2018, six months after the visit of Prime Minister Netanyahu to India, during which he toured a waste water treatment plant. The Gujarat government, in May 2018, promulgated a policy for treatment of waste water, building on the 2017 'Gujarat State Policy for Promotion of Waste Water Recycle and Reuse'. The policy document notes that nearly 60 per cent of the area of the state is water-stressed, with all of the state's perennial rivers located in the southern part of the state. The policy aims to achieve the target of 100 per cent of reuse of treated waste water (TWW) by 2030.[59]

Apart from meeting the potable and non-potable water requirements of India's cities, Israeli companies like the IDE have been active in setting up desalination plants for use by industrial units of big companies. Reports noted that such plans have been set up by big private sector players like Reliance Industries at their Jamnagar and Kakinada units as well as by public sector enterprises such as the Nuclear Power Corporation of India Limited (NPCIL) at Kudankulam.[60]

India is also making use of such innovative technologies like the Gal Mobile, a mobile water desalination jeep, which was handed over to the country's border guarding force, the Border Security Force (BSF), in January 2018. The vehicle can purify up to 20,000 litres of water per day and was showcased to Prime Minister Modi during his historic visit to Israel in July 2017. The Israeli Embassy, meanwhile, is perhaps the only mission to have a dedicated official to look after issues of water cooperation between the two countries, when Lior Assaf was appointed as the first Water Attache.

The use of the Israeli drip irrigation technology is another step by which Indian agriculture is aiming to reduce the quantum and volume of water use. These techniques are being used, in varying degrees by farmers across the country, since the time full-fledged diplomatic relations were established. Israeli Envoy Ron Malka, noted in a 2019 Op-Ed that 32 Israeli-led water projects were being implemented in 13 Indian states.[61] The Union Jal Shakti Minister, Gajendra Singh Shekhawat, visited the flagship Israeli water networking event, the World Water Technology and Environmental Control Conference and Exhibition (WATEC), in 2019 to take forward his Ministry's ongoing cooperation with the Israeli agencies in the critical areas of water reuse, rejuvenation and re-cycling, waste water treatment.

The Government of India started a huge mission, the National Mission for Clean Ganga, under the Ministry of Jal Shakti, of the Ministry of Water Resources, River Development and Ganga Rejuvenation, in 2014. The integrated conservation mission, the Namami Gange Programme, began with budget earmarked for projects estimated to cost over Rs 20,000 crores. From 2014-15 till October 2021, over Rs 15,000 crore have been spent on the projects relating to the programme, including treatment of sewerage water, river front development and industrial affluent monitoring.[62] Since the gargantuan endeavour began, Israel has offered to share its expertise and technical know-how.[63] Israeli officials have met Uttar Pradesh officials and political leadership over the past many years, but Israeli companies are not involved, as yet, in specific programmes of the Ganga mission.

Israel, though, has inked a Memorandum of Understanding with the Uttar Pradesh government regarding water management in the Bundelkand region in August 2020, as part of the India-Israel Bundelkhand Water Project. Israeli expertise will be used for improving agricultural practices and in adoption of drip irrigation methods. The two-year project, which could be extended further, aims to address the water problems of the parched area. Reports note that the drip irrigation systems provided by the Israeli company, Netafim, are being actively used to ameliorate the persistent drought conditions of the region.[64]

Netafim is also involved in multiple projects in India, including in Andhra Pradesh, Karnataka, Maharashtra, among other states.

Indian companies like Jain Irrigation Systems in 2007 acquired the Israeli company, NaanDan for a 50 per cent stake, which later became 100 per cent owned by the Indian company in 2012. NaanDan has been the pioneer in drip irrigation systems for over 50 years and NaanDanJain has a worldwide presence. Reports in January 2020, though, noted that the Indian owner was looking to sell the entire company or part of it to a buyer given the large debts they had incurred on account of their expansion projects.[65]

Space Cooperation

As noted in the introductory chapter, India and Israel signed three agreements relating to space cooperation during the visit of Prime Minister Modi. These included joint research on atomic clocks, geo-synchronous earth orbit (GEO)-low earth orbit (LEO) optical links and electric propulsion for small satellites, with the Indian Space Research Organisation (ISRO). The feasibility study on the joint work on electric propulsion for small satellites was completed in March 2018 and a Plan of Cooperation between the two agencies, ISRO and the Israel Space Agency (ISA), was signed in April 2020.[66] The then Chairman of ISRO, K. Sivan and the Chairman of the Israel Space Agency (ISA) Avi Blasberger reviewed the progress of these projects in a virtual meeting in July 2021. Both agencies pledged to cooperate further and appropriately commemorate the 30th anniversary of establishment of diplomatic relations, through a joint event in 2022.[67] Reports note that while the feasibility study on the joint research work relating to the atomic clocks has been completed, work on the GEO-LEO optical links was yet to be initiated, as of end-2020.[68] The optical link seeks to enhance the communication capabilities between the GEO and LEO satellites.

Both countries have a strong record of cooperation in the space sector. India, for instance, launched the Israeli spy satellite, TechSAR satellite, with the Polar Satellite Launch Vehicle (PSLV) C-10, in January 2008. The satellite was manufactured by MBT Space, a division of the Israel Aerospace Industries (IAI), along with Elta, Tadiran Spectralink and Rafael. A key reason why Israel found it useful to launch its satellite by the Indian space launch vehicle was to overcome some of the drawbacks associated with its sole satellite launch station, at the Palmachim range. Israel has to launch satellites westwards over the Mediterranean Sea, from Palmachim, located near Tel Aviv, to prevent debris falling over civilian areas. Israel had also faced problems with its indigenous Shavit launcher, and has also lost satellites like Ofek-4 in 1998 and Ofek-6 in 2006.

Prior to the launch of the Israeli Polaris satellite, ISRO's first commercial launch involving a foreign satellite was that of the Italian satellite, Agile, in April 2007. Reports noted that the economics of the launch with the Indian launcher would have been another factor that guided the Israeli decision, given that the PSLV was nearly three to four times cheaper than the Shavit launcher.[69]

Prior to the TechSAR launch, ISRO and the ISA had signed another agreement in December 2003 to launch the Tel Aviv University Ultra-Violet Experiment (TAUVEX) satellite on board the Ge-Synchronous Satellite Launch Vehicle (GSLV), with an initial date set for 2005. TAUVEX was a collaborative endeavour between the TAU and the Indian Institute of Astrophysics, Bangalore. The December 2003 MoU followed the signing of a cooperative agreement between ISRO and the ISA in October 2002.[70] The TAUVEX launch, however, encountered delays, and the launch date slipped to 2008 and subsequently to 2009.

The satellite was integrated onto the GSLV launcher but was later dismounted, two months ahead of the launch, in April 2010. The GSLV mission, though, was lost on account of the failure of the rocket's third stage motors. Alternatively, a launch by the PSLV was considered in order to make optimum use of the ultra-violet band telescopes of the TAUVEX.[71] Israel's Ministry of Science and Technology, in a statement to *Forbes* in May 2012 noted that 'the future mode of use of the TAUVEX instrument is still being examined by experts in the field and will be further considered by Israel Space Agency. We hope to have a decision on the matter soon'.[72] Eventually, however, the satellite was not launched.

The TechSAR launch, meanwhile, was particularly significant as Israel was locked in a geo-political struggle with its primary regional nemesis, the Islamic Republic of Iran, over rising concerns on its nuclear programme. The satellite was intended to keep a tab on developments pertaining to the Iranian nuclear programme, among other activities. It is pertinent to note that a few months after launching the Israeli spy satellite, ostensibly for use against Iran, India successfully hosted the Iranian President Mahmoud Ahmadinejad, for a summit meeting in April 2008—attesting to the country's long-standing diplomatic prowess to deal with two important partners, who do not have formal diplomatic ties but view each other as sworn enemies. The Iranian President's visit was viewed by US officials as an important effort by India to convey that the country had an independent foreign policy, especially vis-à-vis rising tensions with the US over India's continuing relationship with Iran, even as regional and global concerns were peaking over its nuclear intentions.[73]

Israel also supplied the X-band synthetic aperture radar (SAR) for the Indian satellite, RISAT-2, launched in April 2009, on a PSLV Launcher. The satellite's ostensible aim was to enhance the ISRO's capability for disaster management operations.[74] Reports and analysts, though, noted that the 300 kgs radar imaging satellite, was developed on a war footing, in the aftermath of the Mumbai terror strikes to plug gaps in the country's surveillance capabilities.[75] RISAT-2 was India's first radar imaging satellite, with the ability to see through clouds and darkness. Its predecessor, the RISAT-1, was a C-band SAR satellite, with constrained abilities, as against the X-band RISAT-2. In February 2017, a nano-satellite from Israel was one of the record payload of 104 satellites launched by the PSLV C-37. The BGUSAT was built by the IAI and the Ben Gurion University.[76]

In the changed regional geo-politics in the aftermath of the Abraham Accords, India and Israel can be expected to further buttress their cooperation in the space sector, with countries like the UAE as well. One of the six areas of cooperation as part of the I2U2 framework relates to space, apart from water, energy, transportation, health and food security. The UAE launched its National Space Programme in 2017, as part of which the Emirates plans to land a rover on the Moon before 2022 and even has ambitious plans to send a mission to Mars in the next century. The country's spacecraft, Hope, entered the Mars orbit in 2021, becoming only the fifth space agency to achieve the feat.

The UAE has in 2018 signed an implementing agreement with the National Aeronautics and Space Administration (NASA) for cooperation on manned space flight. A former Emirati fighter pilot became the first Arab citizen to reach the International Space Station (ISS) in September 2019.

Israel and the UAE entered into an agreement in October 2021 to cooperate on Israel's Beresheet 2 lunar landing mission, scheduled to launch in 2024. The UAE will also benefit from data from an Israeli-French environmental satellite, which was launched in 2017.[77]

The UAE does not have launch vehicles or rockets to place its satellites in orbit. The UAE has launched its satellites from places like Japan, while its first astronaut went into space aboard the Russian Soyuz rocket from Kazakhstan. While ISRO can be a possible contender to launch future UAE satellites, the Emirates can also take the benefit of India's vast array of scientific and communication satellites and the three countries can collaborate on joint scientific missions and experiments.

If the UAE's lunar mission, scheduled for late 2022, is successful, the Emirates will be only the fourth nation to have successfully landed a lander on the Moon, after the US, the Soviet Union, and the Peoples Republic of China. Israel's moon mission failed in 2019 while India's moon mission, the Chandrayaan 2, also failed. India's Mangalyaan probe entered the Mars orbit in 2014, thus becoming the first Asian country to achieve the feat. Chandrayaan-3 is expected to be launched in 2022-23. The Israeli moon mission, Beresheet 1, launched via the Space X Falcon rocket from the US in February 2019, was the first non-governmental mission to attempt a lunar landing. The lander reached the moon but crashed on the surface.

NOTES

1. Global Innovation and Technology Alliance, *Annual Report 2017-18*, p. 12, at https://gita.org.in/Attachments/Reports/Annual%20Report%20-%20GITA%202017_2018.pdf (Accessed September 20, 2021).
2. Lok Sabha, 'Indo-Israeli research project', Unstarred Question No. 2361, November 30, 2016, at http://loksabhaph.nic.in/Questions/QResult15.aspx?qref=43032&lsno=16 (Accessed September 20, 2021).
3. Embassy of India, 'Israel-India Industrial R&D and Technological Innovation Fund (I4F)', at https://www.indembassyisrael.gov.in/extra?id=1aMAa (Accessed September 22, 2021).
4. World Intellectual Property Organisation, *GII 2022 Economy Profiles*, p. 147, at https://www.wipo.int/edocs/pubdocs/en/wipo-pub-2000-2022-section6-en-gii-2022-economy profiles-global-innovation-index-2022-15th-edition.pdf (Accessed October 20, 2022).
5. Ibid.
6. Israel Innovation Authority, '2021 Innovation Report', p. 11, at https://innovationisrael.org.il/sites/default/files/The%20Israel%20Innovation%20Report%202021.pdf (Accessed December 10, 2021).

7. See Ministry of Economy and Industry, 'Invest in Israel', https://investinisrael.gov.il/HowWeHelp/downloads/RESEARCH%20AND%20DEVELOPMENT%20CENTERS.pdf (Accessed September 20, 2021).
8. World Intellectual Property Organisation, *Global Innovation Index 2021*, p. 10, at https://www.wipo.int/edocs/pubdocs/en/wipo_pub_gii_2021.pdf (Accessed December 10, 2021).
9. World Intellectual Property Organisation, *GII 2022 Economy Profiles*, p. 142, at https://www.wipo.int/edocs/pubdocs/en/wipo-pub-2000-2022-section6-en-gii-2022-economy-profiles-global-innovation-index-2022-15th-edition.pdf (Accessed October 20, 2022).
10. Sanjib Pohit, 'Why India always misses the innovation bus', *The Hindu Business Line*, December 12, 2021, at https://www.thehindubusinessline.com/opinion/why-india-always-misses-the-innovation-bus/article37939966.ece (Accessed December 20, 2021).
11. See Karnataka State Council for Science and Technology, 'Karnataka-Israel Industrial Research and Development Programme', at http://www.kscst.iisc.ernet.in/ongoing_files/June2020/01_Ongoing_projects_programmes/15_KIRD.pdf (Accessed September 22, 2021).
12. Karnataka State Council for Science and Technology, 'Karnataka-Israel Industrial Research and Development Programme (KIRD)', See http://www.kscst.iisc.ernet.in/ongoing_files/Oct2018/12_KIRD.pdf (Accessed September 22, 2021).
13. See Israel-US Binational Industrial Research and Development Foundation, at https://www.birdf.com/ (Accessed September 24, 2021).
14. Shira Efron, Karen Schwindt, Emily Haskel, *Chinese Investment in Israeli Technology and Infrastructure: Security Implications for Israel and the United States*, RAND, 2020, pp. 88-100, at https://www.rand.org/pubs/research_reports/RR3176.html (Accessed September 24, 2021).
15. Ministry of Commerce, 'The Ministry of Commerce Holds Online Press Conference on the Third Anniversary of the Establishment of Pilot Free Trade Zones Including Liaoning', April 18, 2020, at http://english.mofcom.gov.cn/article/newsrelease/press/202004/20200402958016.shtml (Accessed September 20, 2021).
16. 'Trump said to warn PM security ties could suffer due to Israel-China relations', *The Times of Israel*, April 14, 2019, at https://www.timesofisrael.com/trump-said-to-warn-pm-security-ties-could-suffer-due-to-israel-china-relations/ (Accessed September 20, 2021).
17. Shaul Chorev Douglas J Feith, Seth Cropsey, Jack Dorsett and Gary Roughead, 'The Eastern Mediterranean in the New Era of Major-Power Competition: Prospects for U.S.-Israeli Cooperation',University of Haifa-Hudson Institute, September 2019, p. 21, at https://s3.amazonaws.com/media.hudson.org/Feith_The%20Eastern%20Mediterranean %20in %20the%20New%20Era%20of%20Major-Power%20Competition.pdf (Accessed September 22, 2021).
18. Efron, Schwindt, Haskel, *Chinese Investment in Israeli Technology and* Infrastructure, p. xiii.
19. Ron Kampeas, 'Breaking China: A rupture looms between Israel and the United States', June 2, 2020, at https://www.jta.org/2020/06/02/politics/breaking-china-a-rupture-looms-between-israel-and-the-united-states (Accessed September 22, 2021).
20. See Israel Innovation Authority, 'Innovation in Israel 2016', at http://innovationisrael-en.mag.calltext.co.il/?article=8 (Accessed August 25, 2016).
21. Israel Innovation Authority, '2018-19 Innovation Report', p. 54, at https://innovationisrael.org.il/en/report/innovation-report-2018 (Accessed September 20, 2021).
22. Israel Innovation Authority, '2021 Innovation Report', n. 6, p. 24.
23. 'How India's unicorns galloped into 2022', *The Mint*, January 11, 2022, at https://www.livemint.com/companies/start-ups/the-many-advances-made-by-indian-unicorns-in-2021-11641794734159.html (Accessed January 20, 2022).

24. See NITI Aayog, 'India Innovation Index 2020', at https://www.niti.gov.in/sites/default/files/2021-01/IndiaInnovationReport2020Book.pdf (Accessed January 20, 2022).
25. See Ministry of Science and Technology, 'Science, Technology, and Innovation Policy', The Office of the Principal Scientific Advisor, December 2020, at https://www.psa.gov.in/psa-prod/psa_custom_files/STIP_Doc_1.4_Dec2020.pdf (Accessed January 20, 2022).
26. Press Information Bureau, 'Eleven teams of Indo-US scientists selected to jointly scout for COVID 19 solutions', September 2, 2020, at https://pib.gov.in/PressReleasePage.aspx?PRID=1650677 (Accessed September 25, 2021).
27. See IUSSTF, 'Annual Report 2019-20, at https://iusstf.org/documents/35627/42091/Annual%20Report%202019 (Accessed September 30, 2021)-20
28. US Congress, 'HR2596, Intelligence Authorisation Act For Fiscal Year 2016', at https://rules.house.gov/bill/114/hr-2596 (Accessed September 30, 2021).
29. Sameer Patil, 'India, United States, Israel Should Pursue a Defense Innovation Triad', October 12, 2021, at https://www.nationaldefensemagazine.org/articles/2021/12/10/india-united-states-israel-should-pursue-a-defense-innovation-triad (Accessed December 15, 2021).
30. Sanjay Jaju and Mudit Narain, 'How to develop deep-tech Start-Ups for national security', *The Economic Times*, July 3, 2021.
31. Suhasini Haider, 'India, Israel, UAE, US decide to launch quadrilateral economic forum,' *The Hindu*, October 19, 2021, at https://www.thehindu.com/news/national/jaishankar-takes-part-in-new-quadrilateral-with-israel-uae-and-us/article37064989.ece (Accessed October 30, 2021).
32. Elizabeth Roche, 'Israel's Eccopia producing robotic solar cleaning tech in India', May 6, 2021, at https://www.livemint.com/news/india/israels-ecoppia-producing-robotic-solar-cleaning-tech-in-india-11620315658831.html (Accessed September 30, 2021).
33. Israel Defense Force, 'Operation Guardian of the Walls', June 14, 2021, at https://www.idf.il/en/minisites/operation-guardian-of-the-walls/operation-guardian-of-the-walls/ (Accessed September 30, 2021).
34. Efraim Inbar, 'Who Won the 2021 Gaza War?' The Jerusalem Institute for Strategy and Security, May 24, 2021, at https://jiss.org.il/en/inbar-who-won-the-2021-gaza-war/ (Accessed October 5, 2021).
35. Emirates News Agency, 'UAE announces $10 billion fund for investments in Israel', March 11, 2021, at https://wam.ae/en/details/1395302917391 (Accessed October 5, 2021).
36. Press Trust of India, 'India, US and Israel collaborating in 5G tech: Official', *The Hindu*, September 8, 2020, at https://www.thehindu.com/business/india-us-and-israel-collaborating-in-5g-tech-official/article32548545.ece (Accessed September 25, 2021).
37. Press Trust of India, 'Two US Senators introduce legislations to strengthen India-US defence ties', *The Economic Times*, June 30, 2020, at https://economictimes.indiatimes.com/news/defence/two-us-senators-introduce-legislations-to-strengthen-india-us-defence-ties/articleshow/76705409.cms?from=mdr (Accessed September 25, 2021).
38. US Department of State, 'US Security Cooperation with Israel', Fact Sheet, Bureau of Political-Military Affairs', July 30, 2021, at https://www.state.gov/u-s-security-cooperation-with-israel/ (Accessed September 30, 2021).
39. Press Information Bureau, 'India & US hold 11th Defence Technology & Trade Initiative Group meeting virtually', November 10, 2021, at https://pib.gov.in/PressReleaseIframePage.aspx?PRID=1770443 (Accessed November 15, 2021).
40. Ministry of External Affairs, 'First I2U2 (India-Israel-UAE-USA) Leaders' Virtual Summit', July 12, 2022, at https://mea.gov.in/press-releases.htm?dtl/35489/First+I2U2+IndiaIsraelUAE USA+Leaders+Virtual+Summit (Accessed July 13, 2022).

41. Ministry of Foreign Affairs, 'UN adopts Israeli-sponsored resolution on "Agricultural Technology for Development",' December 11, 2007, at https://www.mfa.gov.il/mfa/pressroom/2007/pages/un%20adopts%20israeli-sponsored%20resolution%20on%20 agricultural%20 technology % 20for%20development%2011-dec-2007.aspx (Accessed October 5, 2021).
42. Press Information Bureau, 'India and Israel sign a three-year work program for cooperation in Agriculture', May 24, 2021, at https://pib.gov.in/PressReleasePage.aspx?PRID=1721269 (Accessed October 5, 2021).
43. Israel's Agency for International Development Cooperation, 'The Indo-Israeli Agriculture Project', p. 11.
44. Embassy of Israel in India, 'MASHAV, Haryana Pact for Animal Husbandry & Dairy', April 15, 2015, at https://embassies.gov.il/delhi/NewsAndEvents/Pages/MASHAV%20and%20 Haryana%20ink%20pact%20for%20an%20Indo-Israeli%20CoE%20in%20Dairy.aspx (Accessed October 5, 2021).
45. Press Information Bureau, 'India and Israel sign a three-year work program for cooperation in Agriculture', n. 42.
46. Lok Sabha, 'Agreement with Israel for Water Management', Unstarred Question No. 1757, December 28, 2017, at http://loksabhaph.nic.in/Questions/QResult15.aspx?qref=59730&lsno =16 (Accessed October 5, 2021).
47. See Philippe Marin, Shimon Tal, Joshua Yeres, and Klas Ringskog, 'Water Management in Israel', August 2017, *The World Bank*, at https://openknowledge.worldbank.org/bitstream/handle/10986/28097/119309-WP-PUBLIC-56p-WcmpeProof.pdf?sequence=1&isAllowed=y (Accessed October 5, 2021).
48. Jessica Karayamparambil and R.N. Bhaskar, 'Solar-powered de-centralised desalination plants will become popular', *The Free Press Journal*, September 6, 2021, at https://www.freepressjournal.in/business/solar-powered-decentralised-desalination-plants-will-become-popular (Accessed October 5, 2021).
49. Ron Malka, 'Based on Israel's success story, we want to help India in its quest for water', *The Hindustan Times*, November 24, 2019, at https://www.hindustantimes.com/analysis/based-on-israel-s-success-story-we-want-to-help-india-in-its-quest-for-water-opinion/story-dG8BrpIBsYkH8hurynpyoK.html (Accessed October 5, 2021).
50. Ministry of Foreign Affairs, 'Israel: A Global Leader in Water Management and Technology', at https://mfa.gov.il/MFA/AboutIsrael/Documents/water.pdf (Accessed October 5, 2021).
51. Rowan Jacobsen, 'Israel Proves the Desalination Era Is Here', *Scientific American*, July 29, 2016, https://www.scientificamerican.com/article/israel-proves-the-desalination-era-is-here/# (Accessed October 5, 2021).
52. Ibid.
53. Bruce Riedel and Nathan Sachs, 'Israel, Jordan, and the UAE's energy deal is good news', November 23, 2021, at https://www.brookings.edu/blog/order-from-chaos/2021/11/23/israel-jordan-and-the-uaes-energy-deal-is-good-news/ (Accessed November 25, 2021).
54. Rosie Scammell, 'Israel turns to the Mediterranean to address water shortage', December 16, 2021, at https://www.thenationalnews.com/mena/2021/12/15/israel-turns-to-the-mediterranean-to-address-water-shortage/ (Accessed December 20, 2021).
55. Bhavika Jain and Chaitanya Marpakwar, 'BMC, Israeli co ink pact for Maharashtra's first desalination plant', *The Times of India*, June 29, 2021, at http://timesofindia.indiatimes.com/articleshow/83937808.cms?utm_source=contentofinterest&utm_medium= text&utm_campaign=cppst (Accessed October 8, 2021).
56. Chaitanya Marpakwar, 'Probe Mumbai's desalination plant project', *The Times of India*, August

9, 2021, at https://timesofindia.indiatimes.com/city/mumbai/bjp-to-centre-probe-mumbai-desal-plan/articleshow/85165447.cms (Accessed October 7, 2021).

57. See Chennai Metropolitan Water Supply and Sewerage Board, '100 MLD SWRO Nemmeli Desalination Plant', at https://chennaimetrowater.tn.gov.in/pdf/Nemmeli-Desal.pdf (Accessed October 7, 2021).
58. Press Trust of India, 'India, Israel sign MoU on water management, desalination: Govt', November 24, 2016, at https://www.business-standard.com/article/pti-stories/india-israel-sign-mou-on-water-mangmt-desalination-govt-116112400855_1.html (Accessed October 7, 2021).
59. See Government of Gujarat, 'Policy for Reuse of Treated Waste Water', May 2018, at https://gwssb.gujarat.gov.in/downloads/Policy_Reuse_Of_WasteWaterA.pdf (Accessed October 7, 2021).
60. Press Trust of India, 'Israel's desalination tech helps cos meet fresh water needs', *The Mint*, July 1, 2007, at https://www.livemint.com/Home-Page/fKwXguHdvwQhx2TVFaKc2H/Israels-desalination-tech-helps-cos-meet-fresh-water-needs.html (Accessed October 8, 2021).
61. Malka, 'Based on Israel's success story, we want to help India in its quest for water', n. 49.
62. Lok Sabha, 'Funds for Namami Gange programme', Unstarred Question No: 1864, December 9, 2021, http://loksabhaph.nic.in/Questions/QResult15.aspx?qref=30296&lsno=17 (Accessed December 15, 2021).
63. 'Israel offers its expertise to India for Ganges River clean-up', *The Jerusalem Post*, July 21, 2015, at https://www.jpost.com/israel-news/politics-and-diplomacy/israel-offers-its-expertise-to-india-for-ganges-river-clean-up-409660 (Accessed October 5, 2021).; Press Trust of India, 'Israel can aid Uttar Pradesh in cleaning Ganga', *The Economic Times*, May 16, 2017, at https://economictimes.indiatimes.com/news/politics-and-nation/israel-can-aid-uttar-pradesh-in-cleaning-ganga-envoy-daniel-carmon/articleshow/58705141.cms?from=mdr (Accessed October 5, 2021).
64. CNBC TV18.com, 'Mission Paani: Israel in Bundelkhand, A water revolution in the making', November 13, 2021, at https://www.cnbctv18.com/agriculture/mission-paani-israel-in-bundelkhand—a-water-revolution-in-the-making-11451132.htm (Accessed November 20, 2021).
65. Shai Shalev, 'India's Jain puts Israeli irrigation co NaanDanJain up for sale', *Globes*, January 8, 2020, at https://en.globes.co.il/en/article-indias-jain-puts-israeli-irrigation-co-naandanjain-up-for-sale-1001314162 (Accessed October 10, 2021).
66. Ministry of External Affairs, 'Plan of Cooperation between the Indian Space Research Organisation and the Israel Space Agency Regarding Cooperation in Electric Propulsion for Small Satellite', April 2020, at https://www.mea.gov.in/Portal/LegalTreatiesDoc/IS20B3701.pdf (Accessed October 10, 2021).
67. Press Trust of India, 'ISRO to take cooperation with European, Israeli space agencies to higher orbit', *The Economic Times*, August 1, 2021, at https://economictimes.indiatimes.com/news/science/isro-to-take-cooperation-with-european-israeli-space-agencies-to-higher-orbit/articleshow/84940269.cms?utm_source=contentofinterest&utm_medium=text&utm _ campaign=cppst (Accessed October 10, 2021).
68. Pearl Maria D'Souza, 'Israeli agency to launch 100% electric propulsion system on ISRO satellite', *The New Indian Express*, November 18, 2020, at https://www.newindianexpress.com/nation/2020/nov/18/israeli-agency-to-launch-100-electric-propulsion-system-on-isro-satellite-2224759.html (Accessed October 10, 2021).
69. Barbara Opall-Rome and K.S. Jayaraman, 'Israel Chooses Indian PSLV to Launch New Spy Satellite', *Space News*, November 14, 2005, at http://www.space.com/spacenews/

businessmonday_051114.html (Accessed October 10, 2021).

70. Indian Space Research Organisation, 'ISRO to Launch Israel's Scientific Instrument', December 25, 2003, at https://www.isro.gov.in/update/25-dec-2003/isro-to-launch-israels-scientific-instrument (Accessed October 10, 2021).
71. 'ISRO receives flak for delay in launching Israeli satellite', *The Deccan Herald*, April 6, 2010, at https://www.deccanherald.com/content/62361/isro-receives-flak-delay-launching.html (Accessed October 10, 2021); Ramnath Shenoy, 'Top scientist slams ISRO for delay in Indo-Israeli mission', *Press Trust of India*, January 19, 2013, at https://www.business-standard.com/article/economy-policy/top-scientist-slams-isro-for-delay-in-indo-israeli-mission-109022700137_1.html (Accessed October 10, 2021).
72. Bruce Dorminey, 'Israeli Space Telescope On "Clean Room" Ice For Years; May Never See Launch', *Forbes*, May 22, 2012, at https://www.forbes.com/sites/brucedorminey/2012/05/22/israeli-space-telescope-on-clean-room-ice-for-years-may-never-see-launch/?sh=78780c842efd (Accessed October 10, 2021).
73. NDTV, 'WikiLeaks: Menon says Ahmadinejad played to masses during India visit', December 17, 2020, at https://www.ndtv.com/wikileak/wikileaks-menon-says-ahmadinejad-played-to-masses-during-india-visit-442267 (Accessed October 10, 2021).
74. Indian Space Research Organisation, 'RISAT-2', April 20, 2009, at https://www.isro.gov.in/Spacecraft/risat-2 (Accessed October 12, 2021).
75. V.K. Bhatia, 'RISAT-2: Spy in the Sky', *SP's Aviation*, May 2009, at https://www.sps-aviation.com/story/?id=279 (Accessed October 12, 2021).; Radhakrishna Rao, 'An Indo-Israeli hand-shake in Space', *Institute for Peace and Conflict Studies*, May 18, 2009, at http://www.ipcs.org/comm_select.php?articleNo=2867 (Accessed October 12, 2021).; Craig Covault, 'India readies Israeli radar spysat to eye Pakistan', *Spaceflight Now*, April 18, 2009, at https://spaceflightnow.com/news/n0904/17milsat/ (Accessed October 12, 2021).
76. Shoshann Solomon, 'First Israeli research nanosatellite launches from India', *The Times of Israel*, February 15, 2017, at https://www.timesofisrael.com/first-israeli-research-nanosatellite-launches-from-india/ (Accessed October 12, 2021).
77. Sarwat Nasir, 'UAE and Israel to co-operate on two space missions', *The National News*, October 20, 2021, at https://www.thenationalnews.com/uae/uae-in-space/2021/10/20/uae-and-israel-to-co-operate-on-two-space-missions/ (Accessed October 25, 2021).

5

THE IRAN CHALLENGE

The Iranian nuclear contentions have been the most significant regional security issue of the past few decades. Successive Israeli prime ministers have contended that the Iran nuclear issue was an existential threat, threatening the very existence of the State of Israel. They have mounted a vigorous diplomatic campaign to highlight the negative implications of Iranian nuclear progress on regional strategic stability and for its own security and well-being. Reports also note that Israel, in conjunction with the United States, has waged a relentless covert campaign targeting Iranian nuclear facilities. It has also allegedly undertaken such actions as targeting key scientists involved in the Iranian nuclear effort. While India has always contended that a nuclear weapons-capable/ nuclear weapons-possessing Iran was bad for regional strategic stability, it has at the same time expressed opinion against the pursuit of a military solution to address the issue and has instead encouraged diplomatic efforts.

When the Joint Comprehensive Plan of Action (JCPOA) was agreed between Iran and its P5 interlocutors—the United States, Russian Federation, United Kingdom, People's Republic of China and Germany, India and Israel were on the opposite ends of the spectrum vis-à-vis the deal. While New Delhi welcomed the deal, which was the culmination of nearly a decade's worth of diplomatic effort and negotiations, Israel staunchly opposed the agreement and charged that the agreement in fact paves the way for a nuclear-weapons capable Iran.

India and Israel, meanwhile, during Prime Minister Narendra Modi's historic visit to Jerusalem in July 2017, formally cemented their strategic partnership. Given the above, it will be amiss not to examine Israel's and India's policy stances on the critical issue which has dominated regional strategic dynamics for nearly two decades now, and the implications it has had for India's energy security and foreign policy choices.

The chapter will highlight Israel as well as India's policy stances on the Iranian nuclear programme, to place in perspective convergences and/or divergences in each other's positions. This, it is contended, is significant and relevant, in the aftermath of the withdrawal from the JCPOA by the Donald Trump administration in 2018 and the continuing uncertainties regarding the fate of the Iran nuclear deal and subsequent impact on regional strategic stability.

Israel and the Iranian Nuclear Contentions

Israel has viewed the Iranian nuclear contentions, when they surfaced after the revelations about the Natanz uranium enrichment plant in August 2002 by an Iranian opposition group, as an existential threat. This was on account of the nature of the antagonistic relationship Israel shared with the clerical regime, as well as the Iranian government's alleged support to forces inimical to Israel, like the militant groups Hamas in the Gaza Strip and the Hezbollah in Lebanon. The Hamas has been involved in military confrontations with the Israel Defence Force (IDF), especially so after the Gaza dis-engagement in 2005—whereby Israel withdrew from the Gaza Strip, a decision taken by the Ariel Sharon government.

Apart from the continuing conflict that Israel has with the Palestinian groups, there have been four significant military escalations that the Palestinian territory has witnessed after 2005—Operation Cast Lead in 2008-09; Operation Pillar of Defence 2012; Operation Protective Edge in 2014; and Operation Guardian of the Walls in 2021. Israel has used strong military force to 'restore deterrence' in these conflicts, which were mostly in response to Palestinian rocket attacks on Israeli population centres. This, however, has resulted in significant loss of Palestinian lives and destruction to the infrastructure in the Palestinian territory. As noted in Chapter Three, Israel contends that the primary responsibility for these conflicts lies with the Palestinian groups, who fire rockets onto Israeli territory from extremely congested and densely populated places in the Gaza Strip.

Israel has accused the militant groups operating from the Gaza Strip of drawing financial and military sustenance from Tehran. Analysts note that the Hamas, prior to the May 2021 military confrontation with Israel, had in its possession over 100,000 rockets, mostly made in Gaza Strip itself with Iranian know-how.[1] Iran, more specifically, has historically transferred rockets to Palestinian groups via smuggling networks through Sudan and Egypt. Reports also note that Palestinian groups like the Palestinian Islamic Jihad and Iranian military officials have publicly acknowledged the nature of the relationship in the supply and use of rockets and/ or know-how.[2]

Israel has also taken significant actions to disrupt supply lines passing through the Syrian Arab Republic. In December 2021, for instance, Israeli fighter jets carried out air strikes at the Latakia container terminal.[3] The Chief of Staff of the IDF, Lt. Gen. Aviv Kohavi, told the Knesset Foreign Affairs and Defence Committee in November 2021 that the IDF was 'accelerating its operational plans and readiness to deal with Iran and its military nuclear threat'.[4] This was in the aftermath of a series of airstrikes inside Syria by the IDF. Reports note that the IDF conducted over 50 such air raids inside the country in 2020, more than double to that conducted during the previous year. Reports in February 2018 noted that Israel has conducted at least 100 air raids inside Syrian territory since 2011, when the conflict in Syria started.[5] In the past two years, therefore, these numbers have almost doubled.

The Hezbollah, meanwhile, a paramilitary organization with deep roots in Lebanese civil society, was created in the aftermath of the Israeli invasion of Lebanon in 1982 and the subsequent occupation, which lasted till 2000. It has been involved in major acts of terrorism targeting Israeli citizens and properties, including in Buenos Aires, where a powerful bomb targeted the Israeli Embassy in the Argentine capital in 1992, killing 29 people.[6] Hezbollah was also involved in the suicide truck bombings targeting the US Embassy in Beirut in 1983, which led to the loss of lives of 241 American and 58 French soldiers. The Israeli Ministry of Foreign Affairs (MFA) points out that the Argentinian Supreme Court after the conclusion of a formal investigation in 1999 accused the Hezbollah of carrying out the attack and issued a warrant for arrest for the head of the Hezbollah unit that carried out the attack, Imad Mughnieh. Israel in 2003 also accused the 'highest levels' of the Iranian regime of being 'aware' of the Hezbollah's intention to carry out the attack in Buenous Aires and for encouraging such an action.[7] Mughnieh was killed in a bomb blast in Beirut in February 2008, allegedly in a joint operation by the United States and Israeli agencies.

While organizations like the Hamas and the Hezbollah are seen as extensions of the Islamic Republic, actively working at the behest of Tehran to hurt its interests, Israel contends that once Iran attains the capability to manufacture nuclear weapons, it can threaten its very existence. Former Prime Minister Benjamin Netanyahu often charged that if Iran acquired nuclear weapons, it could give its nuclear weapons to terrorists.[8] Israel has further held that, unlike the Cold War Superpower nuclear rivalry, nuclear deterrence will not work in the West Asian context. Prime Minister Netanyahu's speech at the United Nations General Assembly (UNGA) in September 2012 and to the United States Congress in March 2015 are pertinent examples of the Israeli concerns over the Iranian nuclear programme. At the UNGA, Netanyahu equated a nuclear-armed Iran with a nuclear-armed Al Qaeda. Netanyahu contended that Iran cannot be deterred like the Soviet Union because 'militant jihadists' behave very differently from radical Marxists.[9]

Israel has also held the possibility of West Asian 'nuclear dominoes'—other regional countries acquiring nuclear weapon capabilities, if Iran acquired such a capability and the negative implications of such a possibility on regional strategic stability. Saudi Arabia's nuclear pronouncements add grist to the Israeli contentions. Saudi officials, like Foreign Minister Adel Al Jubeir and Crown Prince Mohammad Bin Salman, in the aftermath of the JCPOA, have insisted that they will indeed do everything in their power to match an Iranian nuclear capability, if it materializes.[10]

Analysts, however, have argued that the talk of the nuclear dominoes in the West Asian context was overblown. Esfandiary and Tabatabai have argued that Saudi Arabia, for instance, faces technical as well as manpower impediments to achieve its nuclear weapon aspirations, if any. The likelihood of Riyadh getting a nuclear weapon from Pakistan was also remote, as the United States was still the security guarantor for Riyadh and will have a bearing on a Saudi decision in this regard.[11] Other analysts have also pointed out Turkiye's technical or manpower resources to pursue a nuclear weapons programme were also limited and that the economic situation of Egypt precludes the possibility of them pursuing such a capability.[12]

While the Iranian nuclear issue was referred to the United Nations Security Council (UNSC) in February 2006 on account of the 'absence of confidence' whether all activities inside Iran were for peaceful purposes, regional and international concerns spiked when the existence of the underground Qom uranium enrichment facility was revealed in 2008. Iran insisted that it was not bound to declare the existence of the facility as it had not yet introduced nuclear material into the facility. Such contentions with the IAEA over the nature and terms of its comprehensive safeguards agreement (CSA) generated intense international scrutiny and added to regional concerns.

Iran signed the CSA with the IAEA in 1973, which entered into force a year later, in 1974. The IAEA had long-running contentions with the IAEA over Iran following the terms and conditions of the CSA. These, for instance, related to such issues as informing the nuclear regulatory body of activities pertaining to the building of enrichment facilities, disclosure of nuclear material or components that it had imported, among other issues. The IAEA, however, did not share with Iran the reports on which it based these allegations. Iran insisted that without access to such reports, it will not be in a position to adequately address such concerns.[13] The IAEA insisted that it was basing its reports on data secured from open sources as well as national reports provided by member states.

Iran's activities relating to 'possible military dimensions' (PMD)—as flagged in successive reports of the Director General of the International Atomic Energy Agency (IAEA) to the Board of Governors (BoG), were particular fodder to the Israeli angst. The PMD sub-title was initially noted in the May 2008 report of the IAEA DG to the IAEA BoG, and since then were a regular feature of the quarterly reports of the DG on the implementation by Iran of its CSA. These PMD concerns related to Iran carrying out activities on explosives testing of detonators, import of nuclear material or parts of centrifuges, connections between establishments involved in nuclear research or nuclear activities with the Iranian military, among other issues.[14]

Iran-IAEA contentions also related to access to the IAEA inspectors to examine military facilities where possible nuclear related activities could have taken place. Most pertinently, these related to sites such as Parchin, where the IAEA alleged high explosives testing could have taken place, and wanted to rule out the possibility of nuclear material having been involved in such tests.[15] Iran insisted that the IAEA was given access to sites such as Parchin previously, and the international nuclear regulatory organization did not find any evidence of nuclear material in the environmental sampling the IAEA did near the site.[16]

Israel was deeply skeptical of the diplomatic negotiations that were pursued to address the Iranian nuclear challenge, spearheaded by the P5+1, since 2006. It has contended that these negotiations were in fact being used by the Iranians to expand their nuclear programme.[17] From 2006 till 2015, when the Joint Comprehensive Plan of Action (JCPOA) was agreed upon, Iran's nuclear accomplishments added substance to the Israeli charges. At the time of the JCPOA, Iran had in its possession close to 20,000 centrifuges, and over 9,000 kgs of uranium hexa-flouride, out of which more than 400 kgs was enriched up to 20 per cent purity.[18]

When diplomatic negotiations resulted in agreements like the Joint Plan of Action (JPOA) in November 2013, the Lausanne Framework in April 2015 and the JCPOA in July 2015, Israel termed them as 'historic mistakes'. This was especially on account of the fact that Iran was given the right to continue its uranium enrichment activities—albeit at vastly reduced levels and constrained capabilities, and was allowed to engage in centrifuge research, among other activities, going forward. There were no restrictions, moreover, on such Iranian activity as missile testing or constraints on its regional behaviour. Prime Minister Netanyahu insisted that the JCPOA in fact paved the way for a nuclear Iran, after the terms of the deal expired, a decade after it began to be implemented.[19] Israel did not believe in the contention that the strategic calculations of the Iranian government will change after it's reintegration into the international system, following decades of severe multi-lateral and unilateral sanctions.

Apart from the alleged support to terrorist activities and financial and military support to terror groups, in Gaza and Lebanon particularly, Israel pointed out that Iranian political and military leaders have been openly calling for the destruction of the 'Zionist regime'. This was most pertinently in a 2011 statement by former President Mahmoud Ahmadinejad, who threatened to 'wipe' Israel off the map of West Asia.[20] While subsequently, there was some debate about whether the Iranian President had actually said those words or that his statements were perhaps misinterpreted, it is a fact that Iran frequently test fires ballistic missiles, with threatening messages scribbled on them.

In the recent past, as in December 2021, for instance, the Islamic Revolutionary Guards Corp (IRGC) fired 16 surface-to-surface ballistic missiles in military drills, with ranges from 350 to 2000 kms.[21] Reports noted that the missiles, as well as drones, took part in a simulated attack against a mock target resembling Israel's Dimona nuclear reactor. One of the missiles that was used to attack the mock target was the Dezful medium range ballistic missile, which was first unveiled in February 2019, on the occasion of the 40th anniversary of the founding of the Islamic Republic.[22] Analysts though note that for any Iranian attack on Dimona to be successful, it would have to penetrate the highly dense air defence measures protecting Israel's sole nuclear reactor and therefore, the Iranian exercises were more a show of capability rather than possible intent.

Iran has also successfully attacked targets outside its territory using ballistic missiles and/or drones. The drone attack against Saudi Arabian oil facilities in 2019 and the ballistic missile attack against an Iraqi air base hosting more than 1,500 US soldiers in the aftermath of the killing of the IRGC Qods Force Commander, Qassem Soleimani in January 2020, are pertinent in this regard. Iran has also been alleged to have carried out attacks against shipping vessels in the waters of the Persian Gulf.

Iran's ballistic missile testing activities have been a particular issue of contention for Israel, as well as for US administrations. Reports noted that in the two-year period after the JCPOA, Iran tested as many as ten medium range ballistic missiles. The Trump administration in January 2017, when Iran launched the 1000 km Khoramshar missile, passed sanctions against more than 25 individuals and entities involved in the Iranian ballistic missile programmes. Earlier in March 2016, the Obama administration had also passed sanctions against two Iranian missile entities.

When the Trump administration exited the JCPOA in May 2018, it specifically highlighted the fact that the JCPOA did not have any restrictions on Iran's ballistic missile testing activities, as well as on its regional behaviour. It is significant to note that Iran's P5+1 interlocutors, in a statement included as an Annex to the July 14, 2015 United Nations Security Council (UNSC) Resolution 2231, which recognized the Iran nuclear deal,

> Called upon Iran not to undertake any activity related to ballistic missiles designed to be capable of delivering nuclear weapons, including launches using such ballistic missile technologies, until the date eight years after Adoption Day or until the date on which the IAEA submits a report confirming the Broader Conclusion, whichever is earlier.[23]

The statement requiring Iran to not undertake such activities, preferably till the time the IAEA confirms the Broader Conclusion, is interesting. The IAEA gives such a conclusion for member states when it is satisfied that all nuclear activities inside the territory of that member state have been determined to be only for peaceful purposes. Iran, therefore, contended that there were no restrictions on its ballistic missile testing activities, in the text of the JCPOA. Further, it was not doing any activities or launching missiles that are designed to be capable of delivering nuclear weapons. Iran also contended that it had pledged, both in the nuclear non-proliferation treaty (NPT) and in the JCPOA, that it will not develop nuclear weapons.

Iran's ballistic missile activities, though, generated concerns and opposition from a significant section of the P5+1. These included the United States, United Kingdom, France, and Germany. Iran's space launch vehicle activities have been a particular cause of concern. These countries termed Iran's launch of the Simorgh rocket in July 2017 as not consistent with Iran's obligations under the JCPOA.[24] Even as some US officials were cited as stating that the Simorgh launch was a 'catastrophic failure', others contended that such technologies could potentially shorten Iran's pathway to develop an intercontinental ballistic missile (ICBM).[25] Iran's other interlocutors, the Peoples Republic of China and the Russian Federation, supported Iran's contention that it was doing these activities purely for its national security purposes. Russia and China contend that Iran cannot be denied the benefits of peaceful uses of space technology.[26] Meanwhile, a report by the UN expert group, submitted to the United Nations Security Council (UNSC) in February 2021, stated that Iran had resumed cooperation with the Democratic People's Republic of Korea (DPRK) in the missile sphere.[27]

Donald Trump also highlighted concerns related to the JCPOA 'sunset clauses' and the ability of the IAEA to enforce the agreement. These clauses refer to the gradual removal or diluting of restrictions on Iran's nuclear activities.[28] As per the JCPOA, Termination Day of the Agreement was ten years after Adoption Day. Given that the Adoption Day was October 18, 2015—three months after the JCPOA was signed in July, the termination day was October 2025. Among these clauses deemed as problematic to Israel included allowing the production of advanced centrifuges, like the IR-6 and IR-8, after ten years. The restrictions on Iran not engaging in research and development (R&D) on uranium or plutonium metal, or on enriching uranium beyond 3.67 per cent or on spent fuel re-processing, would have expired 15 years after the JCPOA began to be implemented, that is, by 2030.

The IAEA's surveillance on centrifuge motors and uranium ore concentrate production facilities would have expired in 20 and 25 years respectively. The IAEA's monitoring of the Iranian nuclear activities, as well as Iran implementing the provisions of the Additional Protocol, would have continued indefinitely. The agreement, though, had strict restrictions on Iran, including the level up to which it was allowed to undertake uranium enrichment, the place where it was permitted to do so (only at Natanz), restrictions on research activities using uranium metal, among others.[29] Israel and the Trump administration, held that such restrictions were not enough and that Iran's nuclear behavior was contingent on its political behavior, which may not change going forward.

As for the IAEA's ability to police the terms of the agreement and to detect breaches, if any, Israel insisted that the IAEA was severely constricted in its ability to do so and was dependent on Iran allowing access to IAEA inspectors. This, despite the fact that the JCPOA had strict process in place to examine places of concern, including through short-notice inspections, environmental sampling, among other measures, available to it through Iran's implementation of the IAEA Additional Protocol (AP). The AP has a more robust inspection regime, than that contained in the standard safeguards agreements that member states sign with the IAEA to enable it to carry out its nuclear material accountancy activities.

The then IAEA Director General, Yukiya Amano, on his part, insisted that the distinction between the ability of his organization to inspect nuclear material sites or military sites was a false distinction, as his organization had the necessary mandate under the Additional Protocol to seek access to any site that it deemed critical to carry out its activities.[30] Further, under the terms of the JCPOA, Iran could not deny access to the IAEA beyond 24 days and had to necessarily provide the access. Israel, however, insisted that this time was sufficient for Iran to cover up any activities it did not want the IAEA to examine.

Prime Minister Netanyahu, in a dramatic announcement in April 2018, revealed the existence of a secret document trove of material related to the Iranian nuclear programme.[31] These documents were spirited out of the warehouse in Tehran by Israeli agents. The material contained information about Iranian activities, relating mostly to a 1999-2003 project called Amad. This was detailed in various IAEA reports relating to the possible military dimensions (PMD) of the Iranian nuclear programme, most specifically in the November 2011 report of the IAEA Director General to the Board of Governors. Prime Minister Netanyahu insisted that the material proved that Iran initiated a coordinated programme whose sole purpose was to develop nuclear weapons.[32]

While most of the activities detailed in the nuclear material trove were highlighted by the US National Intelligence Estimate (NIE) 2007, the NIE had also noted that there was no indication that these activities were continuing.[33] The NIE judged with high confidence that Iran had halted its nuclear weapons programme in the fall of 2003. Analysts and think tanks critical of the Iran nuclear deal, such as those at the Federation of the Defense of Democracies (FDD) and the Institute for Science and International Security (ISIS), though, pointed out that storing an extensive archive relating to material on nuclear weapons research was not compatible with Iran's commitments under the JCPOA and the NPT.[34] Israeli analysts also pointed out that while the IAEA reports had indeed flagged such activities by Iran, Tehran did not admit to such activities and that the material Israel spirited out of Tehran were proof that such activities did indeed take place.

At the same time, it is significant to note that the IAEA did give its final assessment in December 2015 on PMD issues, without which the JCPOA would not have begun to be implemented. The IAEA explicitly noted that there were no credible indication of activities relating to a nuclear explosive device in a coordinated manner after 2003 and definitely not so beyond 2009. The Agency noted that it found no indications of Iran having conducted activities relating to a nuclear explosive device using clandestine nuclear supply network. The IAEA did note though that Iran conducted computer modeling of a nuclear explosive device prior to 2004 and between 2005 and 2009.[35]

When the US withdrew from the JCPOA in May 2018, Israel welcomed the decision by the Trump administration. The administration's move flowed from the long-standing opposition to the Iran nuclear deal by Donald Trump, when he was even campaigning for the post of the president. While addressing an event held by the American Israel Public Affairs Committee (AIPAC) in March 2016, Trump vowed to dismantle the Iran nuclear deal.[36] There were differences though among senior members of his administration. These included his Defence Secretary James Mattis and Secretary of State, Rex Tillerson. Mattis acknowledged that there were some merits in the deal, even though it was not a perfect arms control agreement, while Tillerson admitted to 'differences' of views within the administration.[37] Mattis even told the Senate Armed Services Committee in April 2018 that the JCPOA verification was 'pretty robust' though he did admit that it was a valid question to examine whether the intrusive verification system was sufficient.[38]

After assuming the office, Trump, in fact, certified that Iran was following through with the terms and conditions of the nuclear deal and therefore, continued to give sanction waivers. Trump gave such certifications twice, in April and July 2017. These waivers were required to be given by the US President as part of the Iran Nuclear Agreement Review Act (INARA), passed by the US Congress in May 2015, a few days ahead of the Iran nuclear deal. The Act was passed in order for the US Congress to have greater say in how the agreement was being implemented and these sanctions waivers were to be given only when the US President certified that Iran was not in material breach of the terms of the JCPOA and that it was not engaging in covert nuclear activities. Trump, however, refused to give such certifications in October 2017 and in May 2018, eventually withdrew from the deal.

One of the major concerns of the Trump administration, and Israel, was that the Iran nuclear deal did not adequately address what they termed as Iran's destabilizing regional behaviour. These included its alleged support to proxies in places like Yemen, Gaza Strip and Lebanon. Trump, while announcing that he will not certify that Iran was in compliance with the deal in October 2017, insisted that Iran was not contributing to regional and international peace and security, as required under the terms of the JCPOA. What is pertinent to note is that the JCPOA in its Preface anticipates that the full implementation of the deal over the course of the agreement, valid for ten years, could lead to Iran playing a positive regional role.

Israel, of course, contended that such an anticipation of 'good' Iranian regional behaviour was misplaced. Netanyahu, in his address before the US Congress, even dismissed the contention that then Iranian President Rouhani, who was elected on a platform of moderation in Iran's foreign policies, was a 'moderate'.[39] He stated that Rouhani was the long-time head of the Iranian National Security Council when the Iranian nuclear issue came into international limelight and charged that he had deliberately misled the world about the country's nuclear intentions.[40]

Even as the Donald Trump administration and Israel accused Iran of destabilizing regional activities—like continuing support to proxies in places like Yemen, Syria, the Gaza Strip and Lebanon, the IAEA continued to certify that Iran was fulfilling the requirements of the JCPOA. These included carrying out enrichment activities only at Fordow, and only up to the level permitted, allowing access to IAEA inspectors to inspect its facilities, among other critical aspects. In September 2017, IAEA Director General Yukiya Amano stated that Iran was subject to the world's most robust nuclear verification regime.[41]

There were 18 nuclear facilities and 19 location outside facilities (LoF) where the IAEA had access to conduct its activities. The IAEA Director General Yukiya Amano told the press in March 2018—after the US President had stopped certifying Iranian compliance with the JCPOA and sanctions waiver was not given six months earlier in October 2017, that the IAEA inspections more than doubled inside Iran, to around 3,000 calendar days in the field, from around 1500 prior to the JCPOA implementation.[42]

After the Trump withdrawal, however, when no sanctions waivers were provided, Iran gradually began to ramp up its nuclear activities. In May 2019, for instance, a year after the Trump withdrawal, President Rouhani stated that Iran will not respect limits on enriched uranium stockpile and heavy water reserves. Two months later, in July 2019, Iran started enriching uranium beyond the JCPOA restrictions of 3.67 per cent. As noted earlier, Iran had committed to the 3.67 per cent level of uranium enrichment till 2030. Iran's uranium stockpile exceeded the 300 kgs of uranium hexa fluoride limit in July 2019 and the heavy water reserves exceeded the 130 metric tonnes limit in November 2019.

Iran began to install new centrifuges at the Fordow fuel enrichment plant (FFEP) in November 2019, after Rouhani asserted that Iran will not be bound by any research and development restrictions of the JCPOA. In January 2020, Rouhani asserted that there would be no limits on the numbers of centrifuges or any operational restrictions on the country's nuclear programme.[43] The US on its part designated the head of the Atomic Energy Organisation of Iran (AEOI), Ali Akbar Salehi under terrorism sanctions legislations, specifically Executive Order 13382, after he inaugurated new, advanced centrifuges, in January 2020.

In September 2019, Netanyahu further alleged that Iran had covered up a secret site near Isfahan and warned the 'tyrants of Tehran: Israel knows what you're doing, Israel knows when you're doing it and Israel knows where you're doing it'.[44] Subsequently, when Iran began to gradually undertake activities contravening the provisions of the JCPOA—like enriching uranium beyond 3.67 per cent, conducting research and development activities on advanced centrifuges like the IR-8, Netanyahu charged that Iran 'seeks to envelop Israel … threaten Israel … destroy Israel' and that Israel will never allow Iran to develop nuclear weapons.[45]

After the Trump withdrawal, his administration officials touted the requirement of negotiating a new deal with Iran that specifically required new

Iranian commitments on uranium enrichment and wanted the 'UN standard' of no-enrichment to be re-instated. This was Brian Hook, the administration's points' person on the Iran nuclear deal.[46] Earlier in May 2018, Secretary of State Mike Pompeo insisted that Iran's nuclear ambitions cannot be separated from its regional policies and put forth 12 demands on Iran to renegotiate the nuclear deal. These included stopping its enrichment activities, stopping the further launch of ballistic missiles, declaring the prior military dimensions of its nuclear programme and verifiably abandoning such work, release of American citizens, and ending support to regional proxies, among others. A former Obama advisor termed the demands a 'wish-list based on a pipedream'.[47]

As for the Trump administration officials and Israel insisting on the UN standard of no enrichment, it is pertinent to note that the United Nations Security Council (UNSC) in its resolutions 1696, 1737, and 1747 of July 2006, December 2006 and March 2007 respectively, had called on Iran to 'suspend its uranium enrichment activities.[48] UNSC Resolution 2231, which recognized the JCPOA, meanwhile allowed for Iranian uranium enrichment, but within severely constrained limits on quantity and levels of enrichment.

After the Biden administration came to power in January 2021, there were expectations that Iran and the US will come to an understanding on the modalities of US re-entry into the Iran nuclear deal. These expectations, however, have not been fulfilled so far. Iranian Foreign Minister Javed Zarif, in an interview with the CNN in February 2021 did warn that there was a 'limited window of opportunity' for the US to re-enter the nuclear deal.[49] In the Annual Threat Assessment of the US intelligence community, Director of National Intelligence (DNI) Avril Haines in April 2021 noted that even as Iran has exceeded the JCPOA nuclear limits, she continued 'to assess that Iran is not currently undertaking the key nuclear weapons-development activities that we judge would be necessary to produce a nuclear device'.[50]

The DNI's assessment was pertinently after Iran started enriching uranium to 20 per cent purity at the Fordow fuel enrichment plant.[51] Iran's decision to do so was in line with the new legislation passed by the Iranian parliament, in December 2020, in the aftermath of the assassination of Iranian nuclear scientist, Mohsen Fakhrizadeh, in November 2020. Analysts have however pointed out that Iran started producing uranium metal, enriched to 20 per cent, in July 2021. This activity was definitely not in tune with the DNI's assessment that no nuclear-weapons development necessary to produce a nuclear device were taking place.[52] The European Union 3, in a statement, have also termed Iran's production of enriched uranium metal as a 'serious violation' of Iran's commitments under the JCPOA.[53]

In the meantime, there have been changes at the highest political levels in Iran and Israel. President Ebrahim Raisi came to power in August 2021, while Prime Minister Naftali Bennett assumed the office in June 2021, followed by Yair Lapid in July 2022. Over eight rounds of talks were held between Iran and its interlocutors during 2021, with no progress made. Reports note that it would seem that the US and Iran were negotiating different versions of the deal, with both sides not able to reach an understanding on the modalities of sanctions lifting, as well as on Iran's nuclear and regional commitments.[54]

US and Israeli concerns especially over Iran's enhanced uranium enrichment activities, are peaking. With Iran started enriching uranium to 60 per cent in April 2021, US and Israeli officials contend that the so-called 'break-out' time for Iran to have sufficient material to make a nuclear bomb, was diminishing.[55] The JCPOA provisions had ensured that this break-out time was at least a year, with limitations on the levels and quantity of uranium enrichment. Due to US sanctions on Iran's oil exports, meanwhile, reports note that Iran's exports have fallen from nearly three million barrels per day in 2018 to as low as 200,000 barrels per day by end 2021.[56]

Even as negotiations between Iran and its interlocutors gained momentum in 2021, not much progress was made. Israel is alleged to have attacked the Natanz uranium enrichment site in April 2021. The cyberattack allegedly destroyed a power supply facility that supplied power to the centrifuges and reports noted that the facility could be out of operation for close to ten months.[57] Prime Minister Netanyahu, while addressing a press conference with US Defence Secretary Llyod Austin in Jerusalem in April 2021, affirmed that Israel 'will never allow Iran to obtain the nuclear capability to carry out its genocidal goal of eliminating Israel'.[58]

Israel is also believed to have carried out attacks against a shipping vessel in the Persian Gulf in April 2021 that was apparently being used as a command and control vessel to back the Houthis in the war in Yemen.[59] The attack coincided with the beginning of the first round of negotiations between Iran and its P5+1 interlocutors in Vienna in April 2021, leading analysts to speculate that Israel was actively trying to sabotage the prospects of the negotiations. Mohsen Fakhrizadeh, a top Iranian nuclear scientist, was killed in the streets of Tehran by a remote-controlled machine gun, in November 2020, in another attack blamed on Israeli agencies.[60] The Stuxnet virus, which began affecting Iranian P-1 centrifuges beginning mid-2009, meanwhile, is widely believed to be the result of collaboration between Israel and the US.[61]

These targeted attacks on key personalities and facilities, an essential part of the hybrid warfare tactics being employed to set back Iranian capabilities in the absence of overt military strikes, is in tune with the long-standing Israeli policy of prevention, when it came to addressing non-conventional threats in its regional neighbourhood. The most famous Israeli operation was against the Iraqi nuclear reactor in in Osiraq in 1981 and against the Syrian al-Kibar under-construction nuclear reactor, with North Korean help, in 2007. Israel's policy of prevention has ensured that its regional monopoly on possession of nuclear weapons was maintained.

Lawrence Freedman argues that 'prevention' and 'pre-emption' are 'controlling strategies' that assumes that an adversary employs force to its advantage and therefore cannot be allowed to do so. In contrast to 'coercive strategies' such as 'deterrence' which assume that an adversary's calculations can be influenced, 'controlling strategies' do not consider the possibility of influencing behaviour, once an adversary achieves such capabilities.[62] The Israeli policy of prevention while dealing with WMD threats has been criticized for being against the norms of international behaviour, among other concerns. Israel, however, has repeatedly undertaken such military actions, as it contends such WMD programmes pose an existential threat if they are allowed to mature.

The Israeli clamour for punitive military strikes to set back Iran's capabilities grew louder under the Obama administration, given continued Iranian intransigence in its interactions with the IAEA. Iran-IAEA interactions hit a roadblock, for instance, during January 2011-April 2012, over issues relating to providing IAEA inspectors access to the Parchin facility. President Obama and his administration officials however, opposed the idea of military strikes. Obama in March 2012 insisted that the focus on military strikes was 'loose talk'.[63] The 'pressure' component of the administration's strategy constituted imposing increasingly punitive economic sanctions and the maintenance of a robust military presence in the waters of the Persian Gulf to deter any Iranian adventurism.

After the JCPOA was negotiated in July 2015, former Israeli Defence Minister Ehud Barak told an Israeli television channel in August 2015 that Prime Minister Netanyahu wanted to attack the Iranian nuclear infrastructure in 2010 and 2011 but was prevented from doing so by the then chief of the Israel Defence Force (IDF), Gabi Ashkenazi and Cabinet ministers like Moshe Yaalon and Yuval Steinitz.[64] Ashkenazi reportedly flagged the IDF's operational deficiencies to carry out the task.[65] It is significant to note that despite Netanyahu's robust advocacy of a muscular approach to counter the Iranian nuclear concerns, he encountered opposition from his military advisors like the IDF chief and key cabinet colleagues.

The quarterly reports of the International Atomic Energy Agency (IAEA), meanwhile, continue to document Iran's nuclear progress. In the report of the IAEA Director General to the Board of Governors, on November 17, 2021, on Iran's implementation of the JCPOA provisions, IAEA DG Rafael Grossi told the Board that the Agency's ability to verify its nuclear activities have been 'severely undermined' due to its decision to stop implementing the nuclear-related provisions of the JCPOA, including the Additional Protocol.

Grossi noted that Iran was enriching uranium, at the fuel enrichment plant (FEP) and pilot FEP (PFEP) at Natanz and the FEP at Fordow (FFEP)—up to 5 per cent in July 2019, up to 20 per cent in January 2021 and up to 60 per cent in April 2021. The IAEA DG stated that as of November 6, 2021, Iran's uranium stockpile was 2313.4 kgs, out of which more than 130 kgs was enriched beyond 20 per cent.[66] Grossi also told the Board, in another report on the status of Iran's NPT safeguards agreement, that Iran was not forthcoming in clarifying the origin and current status of nuclear material that could have been used in four undeclared locations.[67] The IAEA DG told reporters in December 2021 that no other country enriches uranium to the level that Iran was doing, except nuclear weapon-possessing countries. He, however, added that this did not mean that Iran was producing nuclear weapon but that the Iranian progress required a much more intensive and intrusive verification effort, which was not happening due to Iran not following through with its JCPOA provisions.[68]

With nuclear negotiations not making much progress, Iran continues to make progress in its nuclear capabilities. Israel's Permanent Representative to the IAEA, Joshua Zarka, told reporters in December 2021 that the nuclear negotiations had reached the 'last stretch of diplomacy' on account of lack of progress in negotiations.[69] With the US accusing Iran of accelerating its nuclear programme and 'slow-walk in its diplomacy', and negotiations in Vienna not bearing fruit, voices from Israel are getting shrill about the implications of the Iranian nuclear programme.[70] Chairing his first Cabinet meeting in June 2021, Prime Minister Bennett called on Iran's interlocutors to 'wake up' to the perils of returning to the JCPOA.[71]

Reports about Israel preparing to strike the Iranian nuclear infrastructure, meanwhile, made appearances in Israeli media. Bennett told the United Nations General Assembly in September 2021 that the Iranian nuclear programme was at a 'critical' point and a 'watershed' moment. The Israeli prime minister asserted that 'words do not stop centrifuges from spinning', clearly stating that it would require actions from the international community or by Israel on its own, to do so. In his speech, Bennett affirmed that Iran was seeking to dominate the region, 'under a nuclear umbrella'.[72]

Reports in October 2021 noted that Israel had approved a budget of $1.5 billion to prepare for an attack on Iran's nuclear facilities.[73] This, even as the Head of the Israeli Military Intelligence, Tamir Haiman, was reported as stating in October 2021 that Iran had a long way to go before acquiring a nuclear bomb.[74] The United States and its Gulf Cooperation Council (GCC) allies met in Riyadh in November 2021 and condemned 'dangerous Iranian policies, including the proliferation and direct use of advanced ballistic missiles and Unmanned Aircraft Systems'.[75] The US and the GCC accused Iran of using these weapons systems against civilians and critical infrastructure in Saudi Arabia, against merchant shipping targets in the Sea of Oman, among other actions.

The US and Israel, meanwhile, signed the Jerusalem Joint Declaration on July 14, 2022, during President Biden's visit to Israel. The US affirmed that it will 'use all elements of national power' to prevent the nuclearization of Iran.[76]

From Israel, Biden went to Jeddah, the first time a US President flew directly from Israel to Saudi Arabia. After bilateral meetings with the Saudi King and Crown Prince, Mohammed Bin Salman, the US and Saudi Arabia issued the Jeddah Declaration, comprehensively stating their positions on regional issues, including Iran, apart from bilateral areas of cooperation.[77] Apart from his meetings with the Saudi leadership, the centrepiece of Biden's interactions in Jeddah was another mini-lateral (in addition to the I2U2 while he was in Israel)—the GCC+3 Summit that included Iraq, Jordan and Egypt, apart from the six GCC countries. Biden also had separate meetings with these leaders, with all sides reiterating the importance of strengthening bilateral ties for mutual benefit and regional good.

Biden's successful West Asia trip is expected to negate the rhetoric of a diminishing US regional role. US forces continue to be present in strong numbers in West Asia, with the Fifth Fleet based out of Bahrain. Biden's visit, while reemphasizing US security relationships with Israel, the GCC, Jordan, Egypt, Iraq, also focused on strengthening economic partnerships and building mutual capacities to tackle common challenges like cyber security, climate change, energy security, food security, among other critical issues. As Biden noted in his remarks at the GCC+3 meeting, West Asia is 'more united than it has been in years.' The US President asserted that the US will continue 'to remain an active, engaged partner' and that it will 'not walk away' for the 'vacuum to be filled by China, Russia or Iran'.[78]

A month prior to Biden's visit to the region, on June 8, 2022, the IAEA Board of Governor's (BOG) passed a resolution expressing 'profound concerns' over safeguards issues relating to three previously undisclosed locations, among other issues.[79] After this resolution, Iran started removing cameras used for monitoring of its nuclear activities by the IAEA, with analysts noting that a return to the JCPOA by Iran and its interlocutors looking increasingly difficult. Israeli Prime Ministers, from Netanyahu to Bennet and now Lapid, have insisted that a viable military option was essential, to roll back Iran's nuclear capabilities. The Iranian nuclear issue, therefore, continues to have uncertain consequences for the strategic stability of India's extended neigbourhood.

India and the Iranian Nuclear Contentions

Given the above unresolved nature of the Iranian contentions—which successive Israeli Prime Ministers have asserted was an existential threat to their country, it is pertinent to examine India's responses to the Iranian nuclear contentions. India, as a big Iranian oil importing country, has been uniquely affected by the unilateral sanctions imposed by the United States and the European Union, targeting Iran's oil exports, among other punitive measures, to pressure Tehran to make concessions in its nuclear programme. The following sections will briefly delineate the key aspects relating to Indian responses to the Iranian nuclear issue, and the consequences for India's foreign policy practice and energy security.

After the Iran nuclear issue was referred to the United Nations Security Council in February 2006 by the IAEA Board of Governors—a vote in which India voted against Iran, Prime Minister Manmohan Singh stated that India's vote was in line with its national interests.[80] Singh added that India will pay close attention to the country's bilateral relationship with Iran, regional stability and India's own security, while dealing with the Iranian nuclear issue. Iran was referred to the UNSC by the IAEA BoG on account of 'Iran's many failures and breaches of its obligations to comply with its NPT Safeguards Agreement and the absence of confidence that Iran's nuclear programme is exclusively for peaceful purposes resulting from the history of concealment ...'[81] The IAEA referral followed Iran's refusal to stop its uranium enrichment activities at the Esfahan uranium conversion facility (UCF), which it had re-started in August 2005, after agreeing to stop such activities as part of an October 2003 agreement with the European Union–3 countries (France, Germany and the United Kingdom).

India consistently maintained that Iran needed to adhere to IAEA transparency measures and cooperate fully to address issues on its nuclear programme, especially within the framework of the IAEA.[82] Strategic autonomy as the main strand of the country's foreign policy was very much evident, vis-à-vis the Iran nuclear issue. This meant that India did not want to be dictated by a third country as regards its policy choices. Critics of the government alleged that the country's votes at the IAEA was determined by pressure from the US, especially with negotiations over the Indo-US nuclear deal in full swing.

Prior to the conclusion of the JCPOA in 2015, India voted mostly against Iran at the IAEA on resolutions demanding Tehran cooperate more fully with the IAEA. These includes resolutions passed overwhelmingly in September 2005, February 2006, November 2009, November 2011 and September 2012.[83] After the third vote, Foreign Minister S.M. Krishna told the Rajya Sabha that the conclusions drawn by the IAEA Director General in his report of November 16, 2009 were 'too difficult to ignore'.[84]

It is important to note that most Indian analysts and political parties agreed about the negative implications of a nuclear weapons Iran for India's own security as well as for regional strategic stability. The only difference of opinion, was on the alleged role of the United States in perhaps forcing India's decisions in this regard. Those espousing Leftist political views, like the *Economic and Political Weekly*, for instance, highlighted the 'global nuclear imperium' and the choices India was facing in terms of 'vassalage' in that order.[85]

The Communist Party of India in a Communique in 2007 criticized the 'rising chorus of threats' against Iran in a crisis being 'engineered' by the United States.[86] Even as regional and international concerns were rising during this period on Iran's nuclear contentions, as examined in the previous sections dealing with Israeli responses to the Iranian nuclear imbroglio, India's policy responses were sought to be bracketed as being influenced by US policy positions. This was especially so in the aftermath of the signing of the Indo-US nuclear deal in 2008 and the visit of President Barack Obama in November 2010 to India.[87]

With Iran not following through on the UNSC injunctions to stop its uranium enrichment activities and show greater transparency in its nuclear programme, the UNSC passed four sanctions resolutions in March 2007, March 2008 and June 2010. These resolutions targeted Iranian individuals and entities involved in the nuclear programme, imposed travel bans and restrictions, froze funds, among other punitive measures. UNSC Resolution 1747 of 2007, for instance, passed an arms embargo on Iran and urged UN Member states to exercise vigilance and restraint in the supply, sale and transfer of equipment such as battle tanks, armoured combat vehicles, artillery systems, combat aircraft, attack helicopters, warships or missiles.[88]

The June 2010 UNSC Resolution 1929, in its preamble, for the first time, flagged the possibility that Iran could use revenues from its energy exports to fund its proliferation-related activities.[89] Previous UNSC resolutions did not specifically target Iranian financial institutions though they did urge member states to exercise caution while extending credit lines or grants, other than those for humanitarian purposes. Subsequently, the US cited Resolution 1929's preamble to justify a slew of very restrictive financial measures targeting Iran's oil exports.

The June 2010 UNSC sanctions resolution was in the context of heightened concerns regarding the Iranian nuclear programme after the existence of the Qom enrichment facility was revealed in 2009.[90] The efforts by Brazil and Turkiye earlier in May 2010 to find fuel supplies to the Tehran Research Reactor (TRR), in return for the transfer of 1200 kgs of Iran's low enriched uranium (LEU) to Turkiye, also did not succeed.[91] These fuel rods were to be provided by the Vienna Group—made up of France, Russia, the US and the IAEA.

The May 2010 deal was not agreeable to the US or the members of the Vienna Group, given that it was almost similar to the terms of the agreement that the group had reached with Iran in October 2009. As part of the earlier deal, Iran was supposed to have transferred a similar amount of uranium to Russia, which would then have been enriched in France before being supplied to the TRR. The October 2009 agreement was reached with the Vienna Group as a confidence building measure (CBM) a few weeks after Iran declared the existence of the Qom enrichment plant.

Iran though did not keep its end of the bargain as part of the October 2009 deal and did not transfer the uranium to Russia. IAEA DG Mohammed El-Baradei in his November 2009 report to the BOG stated that Iran had in its possession about 1,700 kgs of LEU.[92] Iran, therefore, had agreed to transfer nearly 75 per cent of its then stockpile of uranium to Russia. By May 2010 however, Iran's production of LEU had increased to more than 2,400 kgs.[93] The Vienna Group, therefore, did not agree to the terms of the Brazil-Turkiye negotiated nuclear swap agreement of May 2010 given that Iran would be left with more than half of its stockpile of LEU.[94]

The failure of the two nuclear swap deal agreements and Iran not following through the requirements of the UNSC sanctions resolutions, led to the imposition of more punitive unilateral sanctions, from the US specifically as well as from the EU. The period 2010-2015 also coincided with an increased politicisation of IAEA safeguards application in Iran, leading to greater uncertainty and tensions, even as Iran continued its nuclear progress. These unilateral sanctions severely impacted India-Iran bilateral trade, specifically India's oil imports from Iran.

The Obama administration followed a 'dual-track' policy, with sanctions and constructive engagement constituting the two tracks. As part of the punitive measures, even as its military profile near Iran was increased—with additional aircraft carrier battle groups, among other measures, the sanctions pressure was also ramped up, as Iran hardened its positions in nuclear negotiations with the IAEA. The US, for instance, in November 2011 designated Iran as a territory of 'primary money laundering concern'. This was only the second time, after Myanmar in 2003, that the US Treasury Department categorized an entire country as such.[95]

President Obama signed the Comprehensive Iran Sanctions, Accountability and Divestment Act (CISADA) into law in July 2010. CISADA reduced the amount of investment energy companies could invest in Iran from the earlier limit of US$40 million—which was as part of the 1997 Iran and Libya Sanctions Act and the 2006 Iran Sanctions Act (after Libya was removed from the purview of the ILSA in the aftermath of Tripoli giving up its weapons of mass destruction programme in December 2003) to US$20 million.[96] The Act also imposed restrictions on the selling of refined petroleum products to Iran (with a limit of US$5 million per year), as a result of which Indian companies like Reliance had to stop their export of refined petroleum products. Reliance confirmed to the US State Department in October 2010 that it was no longer selling refined petroleum products to Iran.[97]

Other firms which were also processing Iranian oil like the French company Total, the Japanese major Inpex and Royal Dutch Shell had to stop their businesses in Iran. Chinese and Singaporean oil companies that did not abide by the CISADA limits and sold over US$5 million of refined petroleum products were slapped sanctions by the Obama administration.[98] Further, the Act imposed travel bans and asset freezes on alleged human rights violators and urged the president to impose sanctions on the Central Bank of Iran (CBI).

The National Defence Authorisation Act (NDAA) of 2012 eventually imposed direct sanctions on the CBI, striking at the heart of the Iranian financial ecosystem.[99] The CBI was charged with helping Iranian banks already under UNSC and US sanctions (like Bank Melli) for evading US sanctions by misrepresenting or not reporting such transactions. Any foreign financial institution (FFI) that conducted significant financial transactions with the CBI was threatened with ISA sanctions, which included the threat of denying access to US EXIM Bank loans, among other provisions.

Exemptions from sanctions threats were in-built into the NDAA for countries or financial institutions that 'significantly' reduced the volume of such interactions with the CBI. This was generally meant to imply at least a 20 per cent reduction of oil imports and concomitant payment for such imports. By end June 2012, nearly 20 countries, primarily from Europe and Asia, got such exemptions. More than 10 European countries meanwhile completely stopped their Iranian oil purchases when the EU ban on such purchases kicked in from July 2012. After the EU ban, only China, India, Japan, South Korea, Taiwan and Turkiye were importing Iranian oil, though in reduced quantities.[100]

Iran's oil exports and revenues from such exports, therefore, began to fall drastically as a result of US and EU sanctions. India's oil imports, for instance, reduced from over US$10 billion in 2009-10 to about US$4 billion by 2015-16.[101] India though made up for loss in volumes from Iran by increasing its imports from countries like Saudi Arabia, Iraq, Nigeria and even South American countries like Venezuela. India imported about US$3 billion worth of crude from Venezuela in 2009-10, which dramatically increased to over US$14 billion in 2012-13.[102]

Even as countries like India and China were importing reduced quantities of Iranian oil, they were facing difficulties in paying for such imports, as a result of provisions of the 2012 Iran Threat Reduction and Syria Human Rights Act (ITRSHRA).[103] One of the critical provisions of the Act mandated that if the FFI repatriated funds owed to Iran through the CBI, they would be subject to sanctions. Further, the ITRSHRA mandated that the 'significant exemptions' provision of the NDAA 2012 would only be issued every 180 days if such funds are not repatriated but held in accounts within the jurisdiction of the country where the FFI is based. This provision drastically impacted Iran's foreign exchange reserves, as Iran was almost solely dependent on its oil exports for such reserves.

Given that the transfer of Iran's oil revenues through the CBI would attract US sanctions provisions, it led to the creation of 'escrow' accounts within the countries importing Iranian oil. Iran's oil revenues fell from a high of more than US$100 billion in 2011 to less than a third by 2013 as a result of such punitive secondary sanctions.[104] Apart from such very tough sanctions legislations, US administrations also used a wide number of Executive Orders (EOs) to target the Iranian government and entities/ individuals allegedly associated with its nuclear and military programmes. These EOs targeted the Iranian Revolutionary Guard Corps (IRGC), Iran Air, among others.

Apart from the US sanctions measures, EU sanctions were effective in piling pressure on the Iranian government. The EU on January 23, 2012, for instance, flagged the preamble of UNSC Resolution 1929 regarding the possible connection between Iran's oil revenues and its proliferation-related activities and imposed restrictions on Iranian crude oil and petro-chemical products.[105] The EU gave six months before the decision came into effect. By July 2012, nearly 10 European countries that were importing Iranian energy had to completely stop their imports. These included Belgium, the Czech Republic, France, Germany, Greece, Italy, the Netherlands, Poland, Spain, and the United Kingdom.[106] The EU was sometimes more robust than the US in applying pressure on Iran. The global financial messaging service, SWIFT (headquartered in Belgium), for instance, prevented Iranian banks on the EU sanctions list from accessing its services, in March 2012. The US only authorized sanctions against such centralized financial messaging services for provision of services to Iranian entities, as part of the ITRSHRA, signed into law by Obama five months later in August 2012.

The EU decisions of October 2010 (Regulation 961/2010), which imposed restrictions on providing insurance services to ships transporting Iranian oil, negatively impacted its oil exports.[107] This was especially so since most of the protection and indemnity (P&I) insurance providers were located in London, an EU jurisdiction then. EU sanctions legislations also negatively affected the routing of payments due for the Iranian oil imports. India, for instance, was paying for the oil it imported through the Asian Clearing Union (ACU) mechanism, prior to 2010.

The ACU was a grouping of mostly South Asian states through which Iranian oil transactions were channelled through European banks. The EU decision of July 2010 requiring prior authorization for such transactions negatively impacted the ACU mechanism, as the multi-lateral clearing mechanism did not have provisions for such authorization. This decision, along with the November 2008 decision of the US Treasury Department banning 'U-turn' transactions involving Iranian banks—denominated in US dollars, which implied that they had to transit through the US financial hubs in New York, severely impacted the Iranian oil payments.[108]

Countries importing Iranian oil had to creatively put in place new schemes to pay for them. India and Iran, for instance, in August 2011 negotiated an alternate payment mechanism, as part of which 45 per cent of the money owed to Iran as a result of oil imports was being paid for in Indian rupees, while the remaining was held in Iranian accounts in Indian banks least exposed to the US financial system. Iranian entities could use the Iranian oil money in such banks, as the UCO Bank, to pay for goods imported from India, like basmati rice, among others. Given the trade imbalance between Tehran and New Delhi however, Iranian oil money in the UCO Bank ballooned to nearly US$3 billion by March 2015 while Indian oil companies owed nearly $9 billion to Iranian oil companies.[109] This money could only be returned to Iran in the aftermath of progress in negotiations between Iran and its negotiators, specifically so after the 2013 Joint Plan of Action.

After the US withdrawal from the JCPOA in 2018, the Iran nuclear deal has been plunged into uncertainty. The US refusal to give sanctions waivers once again placed Iran's oil importers like India in a tight corner, given that provisions of legislations like NDAA 2012 threatening secondary sanctions on Iran's oil importers, among others, again kicked in. New Delhi faced pressure to reduce its oil imports from Iran. During 2018-19, India bought over US$12 billion worth of Iranian oil, $3 billion more than during 2017-18.[110] Iran, which was the third biggest supplier of oil to India in January 2018, occupied the seventh position by January 2019.[111] In May 2019, the Indian Ambassador to the US, Harsh Vardhan Shringla asserted that India stopped importing Iranian oil.[112]

India voted mostly in favour of IAEA resolutions censuring Iran or requiring it to cooperate more fully with the IAEA, prior to the JCPOA. In the aftermath of the Trump withdrawal, the IAEA Board of Governors has passed two resolutions, in June 2020 and June 2022. Twenty-five out of the 35 members of the Board voted in favour of the 2020 resolution while 30 voted in favour on the 2022 resolution. India, however, abstained on both these resolutions, along with Azerbaijan, Libya, Mongolia, Niger, Pakistan, South Africa, and Thailand.[113] These resolutions were passed in the light of alleged Iranian non-cooperation in addressing issues relating to possible undeclared nuclear activities.[114]

Iran, on its part, urged its European interlocutors to step up and not only continue implementing the JCPOA but provide alternate payment mechanisms for its oil exports. France, along with the UK and Germany, did create the Instrument for Trade Exchanges (INSTEX), after the Trump withdrawal but the US administration has been adamant that if such mechanisms are used for paying for Iranian oil, they would also be subject to US secondary sanctions.[115] INSTEX, with more than 15 countries as members, conducted its first successful transaction in March 2020, which involved the transfer of medical devices to Iran.[116] Analysts though note that despite being of limited economical worth to Iran as long as it does not include oil transactions within its permit, the mechanism was a political message to the Trump administration of Europe's opposition to its unilateral policy decisions as regards the JCPOA.[117]

Table 1 captures the decrease in volume of India's oil imports from Iran since 2010, when UNSC Resolution 1929 was passed, which led to the imposition of unilateral sanctions by the US and the EU targeting Iran's oil exports. India was importing nearly 9 per cent of its total energy requirements from Iran in 2010-11, which fell below 5 per cent by the time the JCPOA was negotiated in 2015. India's oil imports again picked up after the JCPOA to reach nearly 10 per cent in 2016-17 but again fell back drastically to nearly zero, in the aftermath of the Trump withdrawal. As Table II shows, Iran's share in India's total trade fell drastically from 2.2 per cent in 2010-11 to 0.18 per cent in 2021-22.

Table 4: India-Iran Oil Trade 2010-22 (In USD Million)

HS Classification Code: 27 (Mineral Fuels, Mineral Oils and Products of Their Distillation; Bituminous Substances; Mineral Waxes)

Year	*Oil Import from Iran*	*India's total oil Imports*	*Percentage Share of Iran Oil Importsin India's Total Oil Imports*
2010-11	9,377.88	115,929.02	8.8
2011-12	11,764.01	172,753.93	7.3
2012-13	9,716.39	181,344.63	5.66
2013-14	8,556.95	181,382.56	4.95
2014-15	7,292.13	156,399.98	4.89
2015-16	4,461.57	96,953.02	4.82
2016-17	9,006.29	103,163.16	9.56
2017-18	9,232.61	132,294.61	6.98
2018-19	12,369.07	167,871.87	7.37
2019-20	1,013.52	153,646.45	0.66
2020-21	22.80	99,703.45	0.02
2021-22	86.1	198,857.08	0.04

Source: Ministry of Commerce and Industry, 'Export-Import Data Bank', at https://tradestat.commerce.gov.in/eidb/default.asp (Accessed July 25, 2022).

Table 5: India-Iran Bilateral Trade 2010-21 (In USD Million)

Year	*Total Bilateral Trade*	*India's Total Trade*	*Percentage Share of Iran inIndia's Total Trade*
2010-11	13421.11	619584.68	2.21
2011-12	16201.49	795283.41	2.07
2012-13	14945.53	791137.23	1.92
2013-14	15278.51	764605.09	2.03
2014-15	11737.89	758371.89	1.57
2015-16	11491.1	643298.85	1.81
2016-17	12886.12	660209.46	1.99
2017-18	13763.89	769,107.15	1.79
2018-19	17,036.65	844,156.51	2.02
2019-20	4,770.95	788,070.32	0.61
2020-21	2,106.17	686,244.36	0.31
2021-22	1,914.47	1,035,056.45	0.18

Source: Ministry of Commerce and Industry, 'Export-Import Data Bank', at https://tradestat.commerce.gov.in/eidb/default.asp (Accessed July 25, 2022).

Apart from such definitive implications for India's energy imports, India's investments in Iran's oil infrastructure also took a setback. Iran, for instance, withdrew offers to Indian firms for the development of the Farzad-B gas field in 2015. Indian oil companies had earlier in December 2009 signed a Memorandum of Agreement for the development of the Farzad-B and South Pars Phase II field.[118] When the Indian Minister of State for Petroleum and Natural Gas visited Iran in April 2016—in the aftermath of the JCPOA, India and Iran pledged to complete an agreement regarding Farzad-B. The officials of the Ministry of External Affairs (MEA) told reporters prior to the visit of Prime Minister Modi to Iran in May 2016 that a deal on Farzad-B was near completion.[119]

In May 2021, however, Iran announced that it signed a contract worth $1.78 billion for the development of the Farzad-B. The Oil and Natural Gas Commission Videsh Limited (OVL) had signed a contract dating back to 2002 to develop the field, along with Oil India Limited (OIL) and Indian Oil Corporation (IOC). While gas was discovered in 2008, due to international sanctions and changed Iranian domestic procedures and rules regarding oil exploration, not much progress could be made. Reports note that the Indian consortium spent close to $400 million on the Farzad-B field.[120]

Another negative implication for India on account of the regional and international tensions over Iranian nuclear programme was regarding the Chahbahar port development, which did not see significant forward movement during the time that Iran was under international sanctions. India had pledged to develop the port, when Prime Minister Vajpayee visited Iran in 2001. The port was seen as vital connectivity link to Afghanistan and Central Asia, given Pakistan's intransigence in not allowing trade to take place across its borders.

Developments regarding the port picked pace after the JCPOA. Prime Minister Modi visited Tehran in May 2016 to sign a Trilateral Transport and Transit Corridor agreement, along with Afghanistan. Agreements specifically regarding Chahbahar included those related to the development and operation of five berths for a period of 10 years, as well as financial support for the construction of the Chahbahar-Zahedan railway line, among others.[121] This included a credit facility of $150 million for the development of the port. The first consignment of Afghanistan from the port to India was sent in February

2019. India's developmental assistance, of 75,000 tonnes of wheat, was also being supplied through the Chahbahar port.

The aftermath of the Trump withdrawal injected new uncertainties regarding India's engagement with Iran on the Chahbahar port. This was because the US administration stopped providing sanctions waivers from doing business with Iranian sanctioned entities. The Iran Freedom and Counter-Proliferation Act (IFCA) 2012 had specifically prescribed sanctions against Iran's shipping, ship-building sector and port operators. The Act though provided exemptions from its provisions for 'Afghanistan reconstruction'.[122] India's Chahbahar involvement was solely to help in Afghanistan's reconstruction and developmental in nature. US State Department and military officials, prior to the Taliban takeover in August 2021, had spoken positively about the nature of India's engagement on the port.

India Ports Global Limited (IPGL)—the Indian company operating the Shahid Beheshti terminal at the port, has been exempt from the negative impact of extra-territorial sanctions pertaining to operation of ports inside Iran. The Minister of State in the Ministry of External Affairs, V. Muraleedharan, told the Lok Sabha in November 2019 that the US 'has shown understanding of the importance of the Chabahar Port operations for continued humanitarian supplies to Afghanistan and to provide Afghanistan with economic alternatives'.[123] Muraleedharan told the Lok Sabha again in February 2021 that India and Iran remained 'engaged on the modalities of the implementation of the Chabahar-Zahedan Railway Project'.[124]

The coming to power of the Taliban in Afghanistan in August 2021, though, has injected additional complications into the nature of India's relationship with Kabul, and the prospects of connectivity projects like Chahbahar. Analysts noted that India's Chahbahar involvement is a 'dead investment, a dream gone sour'.[125] External Affairs Minister S. Jaishankar told the Lok Sabha in December 2021, however, that Chahbahar was a commercial transit hub and an economical and stable route for land-locked countries in Central Asia to reach India.[126] Earlier in October 2021, while visiting Armenia, apart from three other Central Asian countries, Minister Jaishankar proposed that the Chahbahar port be included as part of the International North South Transport Corridor (INSTC). Russia, Iran, Belarus, Kazakhstan and Azerbaijan are the other members of the INSCTC.

India and Iran, along with Uzbekistan, held the second trilateral meeting (virtually) on the joint use of the Chahbahar Port on December 14, 2021. The participants were informed by the Indian side that after IPGL, through its wholly owned subsidiary, India Ports Global Chabahar Free Zone (IPGCFZ), took over the operations of the port in December 2018, the Shahid Beheshti terminal of the port had handled shipments from over ten countries, including Russia, Brazil, Australia, among others. The three sides reiterated the

> Important role played by Chabahar Port during humanitarian crises as well as in enhancing regional connectivity. They also took note of the increase in transit traffic between Central Asia and South Asia through the Shahid Behesti Terminal, Chabahar Port and discussed further development of transportation corridor.[127]

Israel-Iran Geo-Strategic Rivalry: Responses and Implications for India

Analysts writing in 2004 stated that it would be difficult for India to maintain strategic partnerships with both Israel and Iran for a long time, given the mutually antagonistic relationships these two West Asian states shared between themselves. The nature of the relationship with both the countries, though, was different. While India had a robust defence partnership developing with Israel, there were no defence and/or military links with the Islamic Republic. Pant also rightly categorized the US factor in the India-Iran bilateral relationship as a main constraint.[128]

While the US factor was rightly dominant during the course of the Iranian nuclear imbroglio—with the US pressuring India to cut down its oil imports as well as reduce its strategic engagement with Iran overtly, India has not quite supported Israeli policy preferences vis-à-vis the Iranian nuclear programme. These policy preferences related to Israel's advocacy of muscular policies, including military strikes on Iranian nuclear facilities.

As noted in earlier sections, Israel actively contemplated striking at the Iranian nuclear infrastructure, to set back its capabilities. Such an advocacy was in tune with the long-standing policy preference, while dealing with regional weapons of mass destruction programmes, which it deemed inimical to its strategic interests. This was most notably seen in its military action against the Iraqi Osiraq reactor in 1981 and against the Al- Kibar reactor in Syria in 2007. Israel has also carried out a series of punitive strikes against key functionaries of the Iranian nuclear establishment and also allegedly struck at key Iranian nuclear installations, either on its own or in conjunction with the United States, as seen in the Stuxnet virus attack on Natanz.

India, meanwhile, was always in favour of diplomatic solutions to address the long-standing concerns. It welcomed progress in the nuclear negotiations, be it the JPOA in November 2013 or the JCPOA in July 2015. When these negotiations did not produce any tangible results for many years—having begun in 2006, reports flagged the possibility of Israel attacking the Iranian nuclear infrastructure. In the immediate aftermath of the Iranian nuclear issue being referred to the United Nations Security Council (UNSC) in February 2006, there was talk about the possibility of Israel using military solutions to offset Iranian capabilities.

The Ministry of External Affairs affirmed that the 'the threat or use of force can only exacerbate tensions in a region which is of vital importance to India, and must therefore be avoided at all costs'.[129] Later in July 2008, the Spokesperson of the Ministry of External Affairs, Navtej Sarna, told reporters that a military option to deal with the Iranian issue was 'unacceptable international behaviour'.[130] Sarna further added that 'a military strike on Iran would have disastrous consequences for the entire region, affecting the lives and livelihood of five million Indians resident in the Gulf, and the world economy'.[131]

India, even as it was against military solutions, was emphatic about the negative implications of a nuclear Iran, for regional stability and for its own security. India's votes against Iran at the International Atomic Energy Agency, were proof of this fact. As noted earlier, even countries like the Russian Federation and China did not vote in favour of Iran in these votes. Moreover, the linkages between the Iranian nuclear programme and the A.Q. Khan proliferation network were too stark to be ignored for India's policy makers. Iran-Pakistan connections in the nuclear realm began in the 1980s.[132]

Iran informed the IAEA in October 2003 that it had procured centrifuge drawings with the help of a 'foreign intermediary'.[133] Pakistan also gave Iran 'bomb-related drawings' and suppliers list for nuclear-material procurement.[134] Iran's Foreign Minister Kamal Kharazzi, visiting the Pakistani capital after the 1998 nuclear tests by the South Asian neighbours, appreciated the fact that a 'fellow Islamic nation' knew how to make the atomic bomb.[135] As K. Subrahmanyam wrote in 2005, 'a vote for Iran' was a 'yes vote for Khan'.[136] He emphasized that if Iran went nuclear, it would destabilize West Asia, stoke Saudi Arabian proliferation and provoke a counter-vailing Israeli reaction.[137] Iran also opposed the 2008 Indo-US nuclear deal.[138]

When India voted against Iran in the November 2009 IAEA resolution—passed in the aftermath of the disclosure of the Qom enrichment facility, in its Explanation of Vote, India affirmed that the conclusions drawn by the IAEA DG in his report submitted to the BoG were 'difficult to ignore'. The Explanation points out that the IAEA DG noted that Iran's 'late declaration' of the Qom facility 'reduces confidence in the absence of other nuclear facilities under construction in Iran which have not been declared to the Agency'.[139] At the same time, India affirmed the importance of negotiations to find a mutually acceptable solution to the issue, even as it upheld Iran's 'right and obligations' as a member of the NPT on peaceful uses of nuclear energy.

The then Joint Secretary (Americas) in the MEA, S. Jaishankar—and currently India's External Affairs Minister, had described India's position on the Iran nuclear issue vis-à-vis the US as that of a 'man in the middle'.[140] It would not be amiss to characterize India's position on the issue vis-à-vis Israel on similar lines, as even as India actively opposed Israeli policy preferences, it took principled positions opposing Iran at the IAEA and urged it to more fully cooperate with the international nuclear regulatory authority.

After the JCPOA, Indian analysts pointed out that it would expand the scope for Indian engagement with the greater Middle East and provide opportunities on a range of issues like Afghanistan and energy security. Rajamohan, for instance, noted that while India's engagement was 'heavily tilted towards the Arab Gulf and Israel', with the US-Iran nuclear rapproachment, it would have to devote greater attention and break away from viewing the region through an ideological prism and domestic political constituencies.'[141] He rightly flags the possibilities of Saudi Arabia and Israel—America's traditional allies, taking steps to deal with the consequences of Iran's new found status in the region. The new US administration, though, went back on America's commitments negotiated as part of a multi-lateral agreement over the course of a decade. As pointed out in the previous sections, after the Trump withdrawal, India's regional policy options became constricted—on aspects of energy security and connectivity.

India, though, continued with its dynamic regional engagement. After the Modi government came to power, for instance, there has been a heightened political engagement with the region, as evidenced by the visits of Prime Minister Modi to the United Arab Emirates (UAE) in August 2015 and February 2018, the historic visit to Israel in July 2017, visits to Palestine and Oman in February 2018. After hosting Prime Minister Netanyahu in January 2018, India also hosted President Hassan Rouhani, in February 2018. Just prior to Netanyahu's visit, India had also hosted the Iranian Transport Minister Abbas Akhoundi. India's Transport Minister, Nitin Gadkari, went to Tehran to attend the swearing-in ceremony of President Rouhani. Modi had also visited Iran in May 2016, in the aftermath of the JCPOA, for signing the Trilateral Agreement on Chahbahar with Afghanistan. During Rouhani's visit, India and Iran had pledged to enhance energy cooperation, including reaching an appropriate agreement on Farzad-B gas field. As noted earlier, however, Iran gave the contract for this field to Petropars in May 2021.

When Netanyahu visited Delhi in January 2018—which was in the aftermath of Trump refusing to certify Iranian compliance with the JCPOA in October 2017, it was expected that he would publicly make his case against Iranian regional policies in general and its nuclear programme in particular, to the Indian media and political leaders—as was his wont in foreign capitals. After all, the then Israeli prime minister's main burden while interacting with foreign media or political leaders—especially while in P5+1 countries like Washington, is to drive home the point about the negative implications of the JCPOA and Iran's malign regional influence. In New Delhi, however, there were no public utterances on Iran by Netanyahu. Israeli media reports cited the Israeli prime minister as stating that the Iran issue was discussed in closed door meetings with the Indian leadership.

This could be explained, at one level, as an acknowledgment by the Israeli prime minister of the fact that India does not have a role to play in the Iran nuclear negotiations, as it is not a member of the United Nations Security Council. At another level, perhaps, it is also an acknowledgement of the limited options for India as far its energy security relationship with Iran concerned, given that it would in any case be negatively impacted due to the lack of sanctions waivers by the Trump administration on Iran's oil exports. Foreign Secretary Vijay Gokhale, while briefing the Indian media on the January 2018 visit of the Israeli prime minister, told them that 'there was no specific discussion on the Iran nuclear deal in any specific manner'.[142] It is important to highlight that critical and opposing views held on Iran's regional role or on the process to address Iranian nuclear concerns have not significantly impacted in a negative manner the burgeoning India-Israel strategic partnership.

India, though, was not immune from the implications of the Israel-Iran geo-strategic rivalry on its soil or on its citizens residing in the West Asian neighbourhood. This was most evident in the bomb attack on the vehicle of an Israeli Embassy vehicle carrying the wife of an Israeli diplomat in February 2012. This attack was blamed on Iran by Prime Minister Netanyahu, who charged that Iran was the 'largest exporter of terrorism in the world'.[143] The attack in New Delhi coincided with similar attacks in Georgia and Bangkok. Four Iranians—Houshang Afshar Irani, Mohammad Reza Abolghasemi, Syed Ali Mahdiansadr and Sedaghatzadeh Masoud, were identified as suspects in the New Delhi attack and Red Corner notices were issued for their arrest.[144]

While Sedaghatzadeh was arrested by Malaysian authorities after the attack, the other three persons are ostensibly in Iran. A two-member team of the Delhi Police visited Iran in August 2012 but did not make progress.[145] An Indian national, Syed Mohammed Kazmi was also arrested in March 2012 but was later granted bail by the Supreme Court in October 2012. Two Iranians were convicted in early 2014 for the attack in the Thai capital, Bangkok, an attack that took place a day after the New Delhi incident in February 2014.[146]

While analysts noted that the India-Israel bilateral relations were strong and such indents were a reflection of the Iran-Israel 'Cold War', the fact that the attack took place within a few meters of the residence of the prime minster, was audacious.[147] It is significant to note that the attack on the Israeli Embassy vehicle, by a magnetic bomb attached to the vehicle by a two-wheeler borne assailant, took place a few days after an Iranian nuclear scientist, Mustafa

Ahmadi Roshan, was killed on the streets of Tehran in a similar manner.[148] Roshan was a Deputy Director at the Natanz uranium enrichment plant.

On January 29, 2021, meanwhile—the 29th anniversary of the establishment of diplomatic relations between India and Israel, another crude bomb went off outside the Israeli Embassy. Four students from Kargil were arrested for the act, with prosecutors arguing that the accused were supporters of the Islamic Revolutionary Guards Corps (IRGC) and that they had posted objectionable material on Israel on social media. Reports noted that the Judge told the prosecutors that the IRGC was not a 'terrorist' organization, and granted bail to the four accused persons.[149] A letter was found at the site of the bomb blast, which vowed revenge for the death of IRGC-Qods Force Commander Qassem Soleimani and Abu Mehendi Al Muhandis—both of whom were killed in a US drone attack in January 2020 in Baghdad, and for the death of nuclear scientist, Mohsen Fakhrizadeh, killed in Tehran in November 2020.[150] Foreign Minister S. Jaishankar assured full protection to the Israeli diplomats while Prime Minister Modi also had a telephonic conversation with Prime Minister Netanyahu.

India, therefore, was the setting for targeted attacks against Israeli diplomats and the Embassy, by alleged Iranian agents/sympathisers, in the immediate aftermath of the targeted killing of key Iranian nuclear scientists, allegedly by Israel. The sharp exchange between the new Israeli Ambassador, Naor Gilon and his Iranian counterpart in November 2021, after Gilon described Iran as the 'biggest destabilizer' in the region, was another manifestation of the Iran-Israel strategic rivalry occupying newsprint in New Delhi. The Iranian Embassy described the remarks as the 'childish' remarks of an 'evil-minded Zionist entity'.[151]

Indian citizens living in West Asia have also been victims of the regional geo-strategic struggle between Iran and the Arab Gulf states. In January 2022, for instance, two Indians were among those killed in a drone attack near an oil facility in Abu Dhabi, blamed on the Iranian-backed Houthis. Earlier in July 2012, two Indian sailors were killed by the US Navy, after the boat in which these sailors were ignored warnings to slow down.[152]

NOTES

1. Seth J. Frantzman, 'Israel-Hamas War Showcased Iran's Rocket Threat', *Bloomberg*, May 22, 2021, at https://www.bloomberg.com/opinion/articles/2021-05-22/israel-hamas-war-in-gaza-showcased-iran-s-rocket-threat (Accessed June 20, 2021).
2. Fabian Hinz, 'Iran Transfers Rockets to Palestinian Groups', *The Wilson Center*, May 19, 2021, at https://www.wilsoncenter.org/article/irans-rockets-palestinian-groups (Accessed June 20, 2021).
3. 'Syria blames Israel for rare air strike on main port of Latakia', *BBC*, December 7, 2021, at https://www.bbc.com/news/world-middle-east-59561148 (Accessed December 10, 2021).
4. Anna Ahronheim, 'Israel ups airstrikes in Syria as next step against Iran', *The Times of Israel*, November 10, 2021, at https://www.jpost.com/middle-east/israel-ups-airstrikes-in-syria-684591 (Accessed December 10, 2021).
5. 'Syria war: Israel "strikes Damascus military complex"', *BBC*, February 7, 2018, at https://www.bbc.com/news/world-middle-east-42973662 (Accessed October 20, 2021).
6. The wife of the former Israeli Ambassador to India from 2014-18, Daniel Carmon, who was posted to the Israeli Embassy capital at that time, was also one of the victims of that terrorist attack.
7. Ministry of Foreign Affairs, 'Israel marks the 29th anniversary of the terror attack on the Israeli Embassy in Buenos Aires', March 17, 2021, at https://mfa.gov.il/MFA/ForeignPolicy/Terrorism/Hizbullah/Pages/Israel-marks-the-29th-anniversary-of-the-terror-attack-on-the-Israeli-Embassy-in-Buenos-Aires-17-March-2021.aspx (Accessed October 20, 2021).
8. Prime Minister's Office, 'Meeting between PM Netanyahu and US President Barack Obama', May 18, 2009, at http://www.pmo.gov.il/english/mediacenter/speeches/pages/speechobama.aspx (Accessed October 20, 2021).
9. Ministry of Foreign Affairs, 'Speech by Prime Minister Benjamin Netanyahu to the UN General Assembly's General Debate', September 27, 2012, at http://mfa.gov.il/MFA/PressRoom/2012/Pages/PM-Netanyahu-addresses-UN-27-Sep-2012.aspx (Accessed October 20, 2021).
10. Patrick Wintour, 'Saudi Crown Prince Warns it Will Build Nuclear Bomb if Tehran Does the Same', *The Guardian*, March 15, 2018, at https://www.theguardian.com/world/2018/mar/15/saudi-arabia-iran-nuclear-bomb-threat-mohammed-bin-salman (Accessed October 20, 2021).
11. Dina Esfandiary and Ariane Tabatabai, 'Why nuclear dominoes won't fall in the Middle East', *The Bulletin of the Atomic Scientists*, April 22, 2015, https://thebulletin.org/2015/04/why-nuclear-dominoes-wont-fall-in-the-middle-east/ (Accessed October 20, 2021).
12. Stephen A. Cook, 'Don't Fear A Nuclear Armed Iran', *National Public Radio*, April 3, 2012, at https://www.npr.org/2012/04/03/149906811/foreign-policy-dont-fear-a-nuclear-armed-iran (Accessed October 20, 2021).
13. International Atomic Energy Agency, 'Communication Dated 10 July 2013 Received from the Permanent Mission of the Islamic Republic of Iran to the Agency Regarding the Report of the Director General on the Implementation of Safeguards in Iran', IAEA Doc. INFCIRC 853, July 23, 2013, at https://www.iaea.org/sites/default/files/publications/documents/infcircs/2013/infcirc853.pdf (Accessed October 22, 2021).
14. International Atomic Energy Agency, 'Implementation of the NPT Safeguards Agreement and Relevant Provisions of Security Council resolutions 1737 (2006), 1747 (2007) and 1803 (2008) in the Islamic Republic of Iran', IAEA Doc. GOV/2008/15, May 26, 2008, at https://www.iaea.org/sites/default/files/gov2008-15.pdf (Accessed October 22, 2021).

15. David Albright and Robert Avagyan, 'Revisiting Danilenko and the Explosive Chamber at Parchin: A Review Based on Open Sources', September 17, 2012, at https://isis-online.org/isis-reports/detail/revisiting-danilenko-and-the-explosive-chamber-at-parchin-a-review-based-on/8 (Accessed October 22, 2021).
16. International Atomic Energy Agency, 'Implementation of the NPT Safeguards Agreement in the Islamic Republic of Iran', IAEA Doc. GOV/2005/67, September 2, 2005, p. 10, at https://www.iaea.org/sites/default/files/gov2005-67.pdf (Accessed October 20, 2021).
17. Ministry of Foreign Affairs, 'Speech by Prime Minister Benjamin Netanyahu to the UN General Assembly's General Debate'.
18. For an analysis, See S Samuel C Rajiv and G Balachandran, 'Iran-P5+1 Lausanne Framework: Issues and Challenges', IDSA Issue Brief, April 23, 2015, at https://www.idsa.in/issuebrief/Iran-P5%2B1LausanneFramework_sscrajiv.gbalachandran_230415 (Accessed October 22, 2021).
19. Ministry of Foreign Affairs, 'Statement by PM Netanyahu on Iran', July 14, 2015, at http://mfa.gov.il/MFA/PressRoom/2015/Pages/Statement-by-PM-Netanyahu-14-July-2015.aspx (Accessed October 23, 2021).
20. Glenn Kessler, 'Did Ahmadinejad really say Israel should be "wiped off the map"'? *The Washington Post*, October 5, 2011, at https://www.washingtonpost.com/blogs/fact-checker/post/did-ahmadinejad-really-say-israel-should-be-wiped-off-the-map/2011/10/04/gIQABJIKML_blog.html (Accessed October 23, 2021).
21. 'Iran fires ballistic missiles during drills in warning to Israel', *Al Jazeera*, December 24, 2021, at https://www.aljazeera.com/news/2021/12/24/iran-ballistic-missiles-military-drills-warning-israel-irgc (Accessed December 28, 2021).
22. Thomas Newdick, 'Iran Rained down Ballistic Missiles on a Mockup of Israel's Nuclear Reactor', *The Drive*, December 27, 2021, at https://www.thedrive.com/the-war-zone/43659/iran-rained-down-ballistic-missiles-on-a-mockup-of-israels-nuclear-reactor (Accessed December 28, 2021).
23. See United Nations Security Council, 'Resolution 2231', UN Doc. S/RES/2231(2015), July 20, 2015, p. 99, at https://www.undocs.org/S/RES/2231(2015) (Accessed July 21, 2015).
24. US State Department, 'Iran's Space Launch Vehicle Inconsistent With UNSCR 2231: Joint Statement by France, Germany, the United Kingdom and United States', July 28, 2017, at https://www.state.gov/irans-space-launch-vehicle-inconsistent-with-unscr-2231-joint-statement-by-france-germany-the-united-kingdom-and-united-states/ (Accessed October 22, 2021).
25. 'Iran Announces First Successful Simorgh Test Launch', July 29, 2017, at https://spaceflight101.com/iran-announces-first-successful-simorgh-test-launch/ (Accessed October 22, 2021).
26. Edith M. Lederer, 'Russia Defends Iran Satellite Launch against US Opposition', *Associated Press*, June 5, 2020, at https://apnews.com/article/40f95ae0d356462ec88493049191da28 (Accessed October 22, 2021).
27. 'Iran, N. Korea resumed missile collaboration in 2020: UN report', *France24*, February 9, 2021, at https://www.france24.com/en/live-news/20210209-iran-n-korea-resumed-missile-collaboration-in-2020-un-report (Accessed October 22, 2021).
28. The White House, 'Remarks by President Trump on the Joint Comprehensive Plan of Action', May 8, 2018, https://www.whitehouse.gov/briefings-statements/remarks-president-trump-joint-comprehensive-plan-action/ (Accessed October 22, 2021).
29. United Nations Security Council, 'Resolution 2231', n. 23.
30. International Atomic Energy Agency, 'Director General's Speech on Iran, the JCPOA and the

IAEA', November 14, 2017, at https://www.iaea.org/newscenter/statements/director-generals-speech-on-iran-the-jcpoa-and-the-iaea (Accessed October 24, 2021).
31. Ministry of Foreign Affairs, 'PM Netanyahu presents conclusive proof of Iranian secret nuclear weapons program', April 30, 2018, at https://mfa.gov.il/MFA/PressRoom/2018/Pages/PM-Netanyahu-presents-conclusive-proof-of-Iranian-secret-nuclear-weapons-program-30-April-2018.aspx (Accessed October 24, 2021).
32. Ibid.
33. National Intelligence Council, 'Iran: Nuclear intentions and capabilities', November 2007, at https://www.dni.gov/files/documents/Newsroom/Reports%20and%20Pubs/20071203_release.pdf (Accessed October 22, 2021).
34. David Albright, Olli Heinonen and Andrea Stricker, 'The Iranian Nuclear Archive: Implications and Recommendations', *The Institute for International Science and Security*, February 25, 2019, at https://isis-online.org/isis-reports/detail/the-iranian-nuclear-archive-implications-and-recommendations/ (Accessed October 22, 2021).
35. International Atomic Energy Agency, 'Final Assessment on Past and Present Outstanding Issues regarding Iran's Nuclear Programme', GOV/2015/68, December 2, 2015, at https://www.iaea.org/sites/default/files/gov-2015-68.pdf (Accessed December 3, 2015).
36. Sarah Begley, 'Donald Trump's Speech to AIPAC', *Time*, March 21, 2016, at https://time.com/4267058/donald-trump-aipac-speech-transcript/ (Accessed March 22, 2016).
37. Jim Lobe, 'Mattis on Iran: Belligerent, but don't tear up Nuclear Deal', November 25, 2016, at https://lobelog.com/mattis-on-iran-belligerent-but-dont-tear-up-nuclear-deal/ (Accessed November 28, 2016).
38. Committee On Armed Services, 'United States Senate Hearing To Receive Testimony On The Department Of Defense Budget Posture In Review Of The Defense Authorization Request For Fiscal Year 2019 And The Future Years Defense Program', April 26, 2018, at https://www.armed-services.senate.gov/imo/media/doc/18-44_04-26-18.pdf (Accessed April 30, 2018).
39. 'Rouhani pledges "constructive interaction" with world via moderate policy', *Press TV*, June 17, 2013, at https://theiranproject.com/blog/2013/06/17/rohani-pledges-constructive-interaction-with-world-via-moderate-policy/ (Accessed June 20, 2013).
40. Prime Minister's Office, 'PM Netanyahu is interviewed for the First Time in the Persian-language Media', October 3, 2013, at http://www.pmo.gov.il/english/mediacenter/events/pages/eventpers031013.aspx (Accessed October 20, 2013).
41. UN News, 'Iran implementing its nuclear commitments, UN atomic agency chief stresses', September 18, 2017, at https://news.un.org/en/story/2017/09/565112-iran-implementing-its-nuclear-commitments-un-atomic-agency-chief-stresses (Accessed October 20, 2021).
42. International Atomic Energy Agency, 'IAEA Director General's Introductory Remarks at Press Conference', March 5, 2018, at https://www.iaea.org/newscenter/statements/iaea-director-generals-introductory-remarks-at-press-conference#:~:text=IAEA%20inspectors%20 now %20spend%203%2 C000,buildings%20since%20JCPOA%20Implementation%20Day (Accessed October 22, 2021).
43. Kelsey Davenport, 'Timeline of nuclear diplomacy with Iran', Arms Control Association, January 2022, at https://www.armscontrol.org/factsheets/Timeline-of-Nuclear-Diplomacy-With-Iran (Accessed February 2, 2022).
44. Ministry of Foreign Affairs, 'Prime Minister Benjamin Netanyahu on Iran's Nuclear Program', September 9, 2019, at https://mfa.gov.il/MFA/PressRoom/2019/Pages/Prime-Minister-Benjamin-Netanyahu-on-Iran-s-Nuclear-Program-9-October-2019.aspx (Accessed November 10, 2019).

45. Prime Minister's Office, 'PM Netanyahu and his Wife Attend Event to Mark the Dedication of the New Visitors Center, Named after Former Canadian Prime Minister Stephen J. Harper, at JNF-KKL Hula Lake Park', November 5, 2019, at https://www.gov.il/en/departments/news/event_agamon051119 (Accessed November 9, 2019).
46. US State Department, 'Special Representative for Iran Brian Hook: Special Briefing', January 17, 2020, at https://2017-2021.state.gov/special-representative-for-iran-brian-hook/index.html (Accessed January 20, 2020).
47. Mike Pompeo, 'After the Deal: A New Iran Strategy', *The Heritage Foundation*, May 21, 2018, at https://www.heritage.org/defense/event/after-the-deal-new-iran-strategy (Accessed January 20, 2020); Jon Wolfstahl and Julie Smith, 'Pompeo's Iran Plan Is a Pipe Dream', Carnegie Endowment for International Peace, May 21, 2018, at https://carnegieendowment.org/2018/05/21/pompeo-s-iran-plan-is-pipe-dream-pub-76422 (Accessed January 20, 2020).
48. See, for instance, United Nations Security Council, 'Security Council Toughens Sanctions against Iran, Adds Arms Embargo, With Unanimous Adoption of Resolution 1747 (2007)', UN Doc. SC/8980, March 24, 2007, at https://www.un.org/press/en/2007/sc8980.doc.htm (Accessed March 30, 2007).
49. Christiane Amanpour and Emmet Lyons, 'Iran is ready for a new relationship with the US, but the clock is ticking, says Foreign Minister Javad Zarif', *CNN*, February 2, 2021, at https://edition.cnn.com/2021/02/01/world/iran-javad-zarif-amanpour-interview-nuclear-deal-intl/index.html (Accessed October 20, 2021).
50. Office of the Director of National Intelligence, 'Annual Threat Assessment of the US intelligence community', April 9, 2021, p. 14, at https://www.dni.gov/files/ODNI/documents/assessments/ATA-2021-Unclassified-Report.pdf (Accessed October 30, 2021).
51. 'Iran resumes enriching uranium to 20 per cent purity at Fordo facility', *BBC*, January 4, 2021, at https://www.bbc.com/news/world-middle-east-55530366 (Accessed October 30, 2021).
52. Eric Brewer, 'Iran's Evolving Nuclear Program and Implications for US Policy', Center for Strategic and International Studies, October 15, 2021, at https://www.csis.org/analysis/irans-evolving-nuclear-program-and-implications-us-policy (Accessed October 30, 2021).
53. France Diplomacy, 'JCPoA: Statement by the Foreign ministers of France, Germany and the United Kingdom', July 6, 2021, at https://www.diplomatie.gouv.fr/en/country-files/iran/news/article/jcpoa-statement-by-the-foreign-ministers-of-france-germany-and-the-united (Accessed October 30, 2021).
54. Steven Erlanger and David E. Sanger, 'US and Iran Want to Restore the Nuclear Deal, They Disagree Deeply on What That Means', *The New York Times*, May 8, 2021, at https://www.nytimes.com/2021/05/09/world/middleeast/biden-iran-nuclear.html (Accessed October 30, 2021).
55. US State Department, 'Secretary Antony J. Blinken and French Foreign Minister Jean-Yves Le Drian at a Joint Press Availability', June 25, 2021, at https://www.state.gov/secretary-antony-j-blinken-and-french-foreign-minister-jean-yves-le-drian-at-a-joint-press-availability/ (Accessed October 30, 2021).
56. Francois Murphy, 'Iran nuclear talks resume with Tehran focused on sanctions relief', *Reuters*, December 28, 2021, at https://www.reuters.com/markets/commodities/irans-oil-exports-are-focus-vienna-nuclear-talks-top-diplomat-says-2021-12-27/ (Accessed December 30, 2021).
57. Patrick Wintour, 'Natanz nuclear plant attack "will set back Iran's programme by nine months"', *The Guardian*, April 21, 2021, at https://www.theguardian.com/world/2021/apr/12/iran-blames-israel-attack-natanz-nuclear-plant (Accessed October 30, 2021).

58. Ministry of Foreign Affairs, 'PM Netanyahu meets with US Secretary of Defence Llyod Austin', April 12, 2021, at https://mfa.gov.il/MFA/PressRoom/2021/Pages/PM-Netanyahu-meets-with-US-Secretary-of-Defense-Lloyd-Austin-12-April-2021.aspx (Accessed October 30, 2021).
59. Bethan McKernan and Oliver Holmes, 'Iranian ship thought to be used as military base attacked, says Tehran', *The Guardian*, April 7, 2021, at https://www.theguardian.com/world/2021/apr/07/iran-acknowledges-attack-on-ship-thought-to-be-used-as-military-base (Accessed October 30, 2021).
60. Zoe Kleinman, 'Mohsen Fakhrizadeh: "Machine-gun with AI" used to kill Iran scientist', *BBC*, December 7, 2020, at https://www.bbc.com/news/world-middle-east-55214359 (Accessed October 30, 2021); Oliver Holmes, 'Iran says nuclear scientist killed by remote-controlled device', *The Guardian*, November 30, 2020, at https://www.theguardian.com/world/2020/nov/30/iran-says-nuclear-scientist-killed-by-remote-controlled-device (Accessed October 30, 2021).
61. David E. Sanger, 'Obama Order Sped up Wave of Cyberattacks against Iran', June 1, 2012, at http://www.nytimes.com/2012/06/01/world/middleeast/obama-ordered-wave-of-cyberattacks-against-iran.html?pagewanted=1&_r=1&hp (Accessed June 20, 2012).; Kim Zetter, 'An Unprecedented Look at Stuxnet, the World's First Digital Weapon', *Wired*, 3 November 2014, at https://www.wired.com/2014/11/countdown-to-zero-day-stuxnet/ (Accessed October 20, 2021).
62. Lawrence Freedman, 'Prevention, Not Pre-Emption', *The Washington Quarterly*, Vol. 26, No. 2, Spring 2003, p. 106.
63. Obama White House, 'Remarks by the President at AIPAC Policy Conference', March 4, 2012, at https://obamawhitehouse.archives.gov/the-press-office/2012/03/04/remarks-president-aipac-policy-conference-0 (Accessed November 9, 2019).
64. 'Barak: Netanyahu Wanted to Strike Iran in 2010 and 2011, But Colleagues Blocked Him', *The Times of Israel*, August 21, 2015, at https://www.timesofisrael.com/barak-netanyahu-wanted-to-strike-iran-in-2010-and-2011-but-colleagues-blocked-him/ (Accessed December 6, 2020).
65. Ibid.
66. International Atomic Energy Agency, 'Verification and monitoring in the Islamic Republic of Iran in light of United Nations Security Council resolution 2231 (2015)', GOV/2021/51, November 17, 2021, at https://www.iaea.org/sites/default/files/21/11/gov2021-51.pdf (Accessed December 20, 2021).
67. International Atomic Energy Agency, 'NPT Safeguards Agreement with the Islamic Republic of Iran', GOV/2021/52, November 12, 2021, at https://www.iaea.org/sites/default/files/21/12/gov2021-52.pdf (Accessed December 20, 2021).
68. Jon Gambrell and Isabel Debre, 'The AP Interview: UN nuke chief says view of Iran blurred', *Associated Press*, December 15, 2021, https://apnews.com/article/business-middle-east-iran-iran-nuclear-europe-ff1b842fef99a5af08cf40ee50994f4f (Accessed December 20, 2021).
69. Patrick Wintour, 'Israel warns diplomacy proving fruitless in Iran nuclear talks', *The Guardian*, December 14, 2021, at https://www.theguardian.com/world/2021/dec/14/israel-warns-diplomacy-proving-fruitless-in-iran-nuclear-talks (Accessed December 20, 2021).
70. US State Department, 'Briefing with Senior State Department Official on the Seventh Round of the JCPOA Talks', December 4, 2021, at https://www.state.gov/briefing-with-senior-state-department-official-on-the-seventh-round-of-the-jcpoa-talks/ (Accessed December 20, 2021).
71. Ilan Ben Zion, 'Israeli PM: World powers must "wake up" on Iran nuclear deal', *Associated Press*, June 21, 2021, at https://apnews.com/article/donald-trump-israel-middle-east-iran-iran-

nuclear-6e9b96c0f7cc414d4996a8d3227fb362 (Accessed December 20, 2021).

72. 'Full text of Bennett's UN speech: Iran's nuclear program at a "watershed moment"', *The Times of Israel,* September 27, 2021, at https://www.timesofisrael.com/full-text-of-bennetts-un-speech-irans-nuclear-program-at-a-watershed-moment/ (Accessed December 20, 2021).
73. 'Israel approves budget of $1.5bn to prepare for attack on Iran', *Middle East Monitor,* October 19, 2021, https://www.middleeastmonitor.com/20211019-israel-approves-budget-of-1-5bn-to-prepare-for-attack-on-iran/ (Accessed December 20, 2021).
74. Anna Ahronheim, 'Iran not getting the bomb any time soon: Military intelligence head', *The Jerusalem Post,* October 2021, at https://www.jpost.com/middle-east/iran-news/head-of-military-intelligence-iran-not-getting-the-bomb-any-time-soon-680853 (Accessed December 20, 2021).
75. US State Department, 'US GCC Iran Working Group Statement', November 17, 2021, at https://www.state.gov/u-s-gcc-iran-working-group-statement/(Accessed December 20, 2021).
76. The White House, 'The Jerusalem US-Israel Strategic Partnership Joint Declaration', July 14, 2022, at https://www.whitehouse.gov/briefing-room/statements-releases/2022/07/14/the-jerusalem-u-s-israel-strategic-partnership-joint-declaration/ (Accessed July 15, 2022).
77. The White House, 'The Jeddah Communique: A Joint Statement Between the United States of America and the Kingdom of Saudi Arabia', July 15, 2022, at https://www.whitehouse.gov/briefing-room/statements-releases/2022/07/15/the-jeddah-communique-a-joint-statement-between-the-united-states-of-america-and-the-kingdom-of-saudi-arabia/ (Accessed July 15, 2022).
78. The White House, 'Remarks by President Biden at the GCC 3 Summit Meeting', June 16, 2022, at https://www.whitehouse.gov/briefing-room/speeches-remarks/2022/07/16/remarks-by-president-biden-at-the-gcc-3-summit-meeting/ (Accessed July 16, 2022).
79. International Atomic Energy Agency, 'NPT safeguards agreement with the Islamic Republic of Iran', GOV/2022/34, June 8, 2022, at https://www.iaea.org/sites/default/files/22/06/gov2022-34.pdf (Accessed July 16, 2022).
80. Prime Minister's Office, 'PM's reply to the Lok Sabha debate on India's vote at the IAEA on Iran's Nuclear Programme', March 6, 2006, at https://archivepmo.nic.in/drmanmohansingh/content_print.php?nodeid=280&nodetype=2 (Accessed July 30, 2008).
81. International Atomic Energy Agency, 'Implementation of the NPT Safeguards Agreement in the Islamic Republic of Iran', GOV/2006/14, February 4, 2006, at https://www.iaea.org/sites/default/files/gov2006-14.pdf (Accessed July 30, 2008).
82. Prime Minister's Office, 'PM's reply to the debate on the Motion of Confidence in the Lok Sabha', July 22, 2008, https://archivepmo.nic.in/drmanmohansingh/speech-details.php?nodeid=672 (Accessed July 30, 2008).
83. In the November 2009 vote, out of the 35-member IAEA Board, 25 members voted in favour of the resolution, and against Iran. In the September 2005 and February 2006 resolutions, 22 and 27 countries out of the 35 member Board voted against Iran. Cuba, Malaysia, Syria and Venezuela were the only four countries which voted in favour of Iran in the 2005, 2006 and 2009 resolutions. Afghanistan, Algeria, Belarus, Brazil, Peoples Republic of China, Egypt, Indonesia, Libya, Pakistan, Mexico, Nigeria, Russian Federation, Sri Lanka, South Africa, Turkiye, Tunisia, Vietnam, Yemen were the 18 countries, cumulatively, which abstained during these three votes. It is interesting to note that even China, Pakistan and Russia did not vote in favour of Iran during these votes.
84. International Atomic Energy Agency, 'Implementation of the NPT safeguards agreement and relevant provisions of Security Council resolutions 1737 (2006), 1747 (2007), 1803 (2008)

and 1835 (2008) in the Islamic Republic of Iran', November 27, 2009, at http://www.iaea.org/Publications/Documents/Board/2009/gov2009-82.pdf (Accessed December 15, 2009).
85. Editorial, 'The Nuclear imperium and India', *Economic and Political Weekly*, October 1, 2005.
86. Communist Party of India (Marxist), 'Politburo Communique', February 18, 2007, at http://cpim.org/content/pb-communique-0 (Accessed July 30, 2008).
87. Communist Party of India (Marxist), 'Outcome of Obama Visit', November 9, 2010, http://cpim.org/content/outcome-obama-visit (Accessed July 30, 2008).
88. United Nations Security Council, 'Security Council Toughens Sanctions against Iran, Adds Arms Embargo, With Unanimous Adoption of Resolution 1747 (2007)', UN Doc. SC/8980, March 24, 2007, at https://www.un.org/press/en/2007/sc8980.doc.htm (Accessed September 30, 2021).
89. United Nations Security Council, 'Resolution 1929', UN Doc. S/RES/1929/2010, June 9, 2010, at https://undocs.org/S/RES/1929(2010) (Accessed September 30, 2021).
90. Peter Crail, 'Secret Iranian Enrichment Facility Revealed', *Arms Control Today*, October 2009, at https://www.armscontrol.org/act/2009-10/secret-iranian-enrichment-facility-revealed (Accessed September 30, 2021).
91. 'Iran, Turkey and Brazil Declaration', *Al Jazeera*, May 18, 2010, at https://www.aljazeera.com/news/middleeast/2010/05/201051795513637980.html (Accessed September 30, 2021).
92. International Atomic Energy Agency, 'Implementation of the NPT Safeguards Agreement and Relevant Provisions of Security Council Resolutions 1737 (2006), 1747 (2007), 1803 (2008) and 1835 (2008) in the Islamic Republic of Iran', IAEA Doc. GOV/2009/74, November 16, 2009, p. 2, at https://www.iaea.org/sites/default/files/gov2009-74.pdf (Accessed November 30, 2009).
93. International Atomic Energy Agency, 'Implementation of the NPT Safeguards Agreement and Relevant Provisions of Security Council Resolutions 1737 (2006), 1747 (2007), 1803 (2008) and 1835 (2008) in the Islamic Republic of Iran', IAEA Doc. GOV/2010/28, May 31, 2010, at https://www.iaea.org/sites/default/files/gov2010-28.pdf (Accessed June 15, 2021).
94. David E. Sanger and Michael Slackman, 'US is Skeptical on Iranian Deal for Nuclear Fuel', *The New York Times*, May 17, 2010, at http://www.nytimes.com/2010/05/18/world/middleeast/18iran.html?ref=todayspaper (Accessed September 30, 2021).
95. US Treasury Department, 'Fact Sheet: New sanctions on Iran', November 21, 2011, at https://www.treasury.gov/press-center/press-releases/Pages/tg1367.aspx (Accessed December 10, 2011).
96. US Treasury Department, 'Comprehensive Iran Sanctions, Accountability and Divestment Act', July 1, 2010, at https://www.treasury.gov/resource-center/sanctions/Documents/hr2194.pdf (Accessed November 1, 2019).
97. Press Trust of India, 'No Longer Selling Refined Petroleum to Iran: RIL to US', October 1, 2010, at https://economictimes.indiatimes.com/industry/energy/oil-gas/no-longer-selling-refined-petroleum-to-iran-ril-to-us/articleshow/6662860.cms?from=mdr (Accessed December 5, 2020).
98. Wendy Sherman, 'Examining the Global Impact of the Iran Regime Sanctions and Evaluate the Effectiveness of the Comprehensive Iran Sanctions, Accountability, and Divestment Act', October 13, 2011, at https://www.govinfo.gov/content/pkg/CHRG-112shrg73564/html/CHRG-112shrg73564.htm (Accessed November 1, 2019).
99. Govinfo.gov, 'National Defence Authorization Act for Fiscal Year 2012', December 31, 2011, at https://www.govinfo.gov/content/pkg/PLAW-112publ81/pdf/PLAW-112publ81.pdf (Accessed November 5, 2019).

100. Kelsey Davenport, 'Sanctions Tighten on Iran', *Arms Control Today*, July 2012, at https://www.armscontrol.org/act/2012-07/sanctions-tighten-iran-0 (Accessed December 5, 2020).
101. Ministry of Commerce and Industry, '270900: Petroleum Oils and Oils Obtained from Bituminous Minerals Crude', November 8, 2019, at https://commerce-app.gov.in/eidb/icomxcnt.asp (Accessed November 8, 2019).
102. Ibid.
103. US Treasury Department, 'Iran Threat Reduction and Syria Human Rights Act', January 3, 2012, at https://www.treasury.gov/resource-center/sanctions/Documents/hr_1905_pl_112_158.pdf (Accessed November 3, 2019).
104. Marjorie Olster, 'US: Iran Can't Access Much Oil Income', *Associated Press*, August 30, 2013, at https://news.yahoo.com/apnewsbreak-us-iran-cant-access-much-oil-income-074343048—politics.html (Accessed November 5, 2019).
105. Council of the European Union, 'Council Decision 2012/35/CFSP', January 24, 2012, at https://eur-lex.europa.eu/LexUriServ/LexUriServ.do?uri=OJ:L:2012:019:0022:0030:EN:PDF (Accessed November 2, 2019).
106. Kenneth Katzman, 'Iran Sanctions', July 23, 2020, p. 19, at https://fas.org/sgp/crs/mideast/RS20871.pdf (Accessed December 5, 2020); DW, 'EU Begins Boycott of Iranian Oil', July 1, 2012, at https://www.dw.com/en/eu-begins-boycott-of-iranian-oil/a-16064179 (Accessed December 5, 2020).
107. Council of the European Union, 'Council Regulation (EU) No 961/2010', October 25, 2010, at https://eur-lex.europa.eu/LexUriServ/LexUriServ.do?uri=OJ:L:2010:281:0001:0077:EN:PDF (Accessed November 2, 2019).
108. US Treasury Department, 'Fact Sheet: Treasury Strengthens Preventive Measures against Iran', November 6, 2008, at https://www.treasury.gov/press-center/press-releases/pages/hp1258.aspx (Accessed December 5, 2020).
109. Jyoti Mukul and Nayanima Basu, 'Despite Deal, India's Payment Issues with Iran Persist', *Business Standard*, April 4, 2015, at http://www.business-standard.com/article/economy-policy/despite-deal-india-s-payment-issues-with-iran-persist-115040400012_1.html (Accessed November 4, 2019).
110. Ministry of Commerce and Industry, 'Export-Import Data Bank', at https://commerce-app.gov.in/eidb/icomq.asp (Accessed November 2, 2019).
111. Nidhi Verma, 'India's Oil Imports from Iran Plunged 45 pct in Jan y/y', *Reuters*, February 15, 2019, at https://www.reuters.com/article/india-oil-iran/indias-oil-imports-from-iran-plunged-45-pct-in-jan-y-y-idUSL3N20A3HS (Accessed November 8, 2019).
112. 'India Has Ended Iranian Oil Imports to Comply with US Sanctions: Envoy', *Business Standard*, May 24, 2019, at https://www.business-standard.com/article/economy-policy/india-has-ended-iranian-oil-imports-to-comply-with-us-sanctions-envoy-119052400105_1.html (Accessed November 8, 2019).
113. 'UN nuclear watchdog's board raises pressure on Iran over suspect sites', *Reuters*, June 19, 2020, at https://www.reuters.com/article/us-iran-nuclear-iaea-idUSKBN23Q1DQ (Accessed July 25, 2022); 'India goes with Pakistan and Libya, abstains from vote on IAEA resolution slamming Iran', *The Times of India*, June 11, 2022, at https://timesofindia.indiatimes.com/india/india-goes-with-pakistan-libya-abstains-from-vote-on-iaea-resolution-slamming-iran/articleshow/92136461.cms (Accessed July 25, 2022)
114. See International Atomic Energy Agency, 'NPT Safeguards Agreement with the Islamic Republic of Iran', GOV/2022/26, May 30, 2022, at https://www.iaea.org/sites/default/files/22/06/gov2022-26.pdf (Accessed July 25, 2022)

115. Nik Martin, 'Can an Enhanced INSTEX Really Work for Iran?' *DW*, July 12, 2019, at https://www.dw.com/en/can-an-enhanced-instex-really-work-for-iran/a-49554580 (Accessed November 2, 2019).
116. 'Europe and Iran Complete First INSTEX Deal Dodging US Sanctions', *DW*, March 31, 2020, at https://www.dw.com/en/europe-and-iran-complete-first-instex-deal-dodging-us-sanctions/a-52966842 (Accessed December 6, 2020).
117. Siobhan Dowling, 'INSTEX: Doubts Linger over Europe's Iran Sanctions Workaround', *Al Jazeera*, July 1, 2019, at https://www.aljazeera.com/ajimpact/instex-doubts-linger-europe-iran-sanctions-workaround-190701095202660.html (Accessed November 8, 2019); Frances Coppola, 'Europe Circumvents US Sanctions on Iran', *Forbes*, June 30, 2019, at https://www.forbes.com/sites/francescoppola/2019/06/30/europe-circumvents-u-s-sanctions-on-iran/#20d890e92c8d (Accessed November 8, 2019).
118. Lok Sabha, 'Investment by ONGC in gas field in Iran', Unstarred Question 5558, April 29, 2010, at http://loksabhaph.nic.in/Questions/QResult15.aspx?qref=87227&lsno=15 (Accessed May 25, 2016).
119. Ministry of External Affairs, 'Transcript of Media Briefing on Prime Minister's forthcoming visit to Iran', May 20, 2016, at http://www.mea.gov.in/media-briefings.htm?dtl/26836/Transcript+of+Media+Briefing+on+Prime+Ministers+forthcoming+visit+to+Iran (Accessed May 25, 2016).
120. Press Trust of India, 'India loses ONGC-discovered Farzad-B gas field in Iran', May 17, 2021, at https://timesofindia.indiatimes.com/business/india-business/india-loses-ongc-discovered-farzad-b-gas-field-in-iran/articleshow/82706202.cms (Accessed May 25, 2021)
121. Ministry of External Affairs, 'List of Agreements/MOUs signed during the visit of Prime Minister to Iran', May 23, 2016, at http://www.mea.gov.in/outoging-visit-detail.htm?26841/List+of+AgreementsMOUs+signed+during+the+visit+of+Prime+Minister+to+Iran+May+23+2016 (Accessed May 25, 2016).
122. The text of the Act is available at https://uscode.house.gov/view.xhtml?path=/prelim@title22/chapter95&edition=prelim (Accessed May 25, 2016).
123. Lok Sabha, 'Status of Chahbahar Port', Unstarred Question No. 513, November 11, 2019, at http://loksabhaph.nic.in/Questions/QResult15.aspx?qref=6948&lsno=17 (Accessed December 20, 2021).
124. Lok Sabha, 'Chahbahar-Zahedan Railway Line', Unstarred Question No.1475, February 10, 2021, at https://mea.gov.in/lok-sabha.htm?dtl/33493/QUESTION+NO1475+CHABAHARZAHEDEN+RAILWAYS+LINE (Accessed December 20, 2021).
125. Sanjay Kapoor, 'With Taliban Dominance, India's Chabahar Port Could Become a Dead Investment', *The Wire*, August 13, 2021, at https://thewire.in/external-affairs/with-taliban-takeover-indias-chabahar-port-could-become-a-dead-investment (Accessed December 20, 2021).
126. Rezaul Laskar, 'India, Iran and Uzbekistan hold discussion on Chabahar port', *The Hindustan Times*, December 15, 2021, at https://www.hindustantimes.com/india-news/india-iran-and-uzbekistan-to-develop-transport-corridor-centred-round-chabahar-port-101639500807544.html (Accessed December 20, 2021).
127. Ministry of External Affairs, 'Second Trilateral Working Group Meeting between India, Iran and Uzbekistan on joint use of Chabahar Port', December 14, 2021, at https://www.mea.gov.in/press-releases.htm?dtl/34653/Second_Trilateral_Working_Group_Meeting_ between_ India_ Iran_and_Uzbekistan_on_joint_use_of_Chabahar_Port (Accessed December 20, 2021).
128. Harsh V. Pant, 'India and Iran: An "Axis" in the Making?' *Asian Survey*, Vol. 44, No. 3 (May-

Jun., 2004), pp. 369-383. Iranian President Mohammed Khatami was the Chief Guest at the Republic Day parade in 2003 and analysts were speculating about the prospects of the growth of the India-Iran bilateral relationship.

129. Ministry of External Affairs, 'In response to a question "We have heard reports that there may be use of force or sanctions against Iran. What is India's position?" April 25, 2006, at https://mea.gov.in/media-briefings.htm?dtl/3033/In+response+to+a+question+We+have+ heard+ reports+that+there+may+be+use+of+force+or+sanctions+against+ Iran+ What+ is+ Indias+ position (Accessed December 20, 2008).
130. Press Trust of India, 'India against military attack on Iran', *India Today*, July 14, 2008, at https://www.indiatoday.in/latest-headlines/story/india-against-military-attack-on-iran-27244-2008-07-14 (Accessed December 20, 2008).
131. Ministry of External Affairs Spokesperson, Sarna, was later appointed as India's Ambassador to Israel from November 2008 to August 2012, a time period which saw a peaking of the contentions regarding the Iranian nuclear programme and significant Israeli military actions in the Gaza Strip, like the 2008 Operation Cast Lead–the first major Israeli military action after the Gaza dis-engagement.
132. K. Subrahmanyam, 'The truth about Tehran', *The Indian Express*, April 28, 2008, at http://archive.indianexpress.com/news/the-truth-about-tehran/302376/0 (Accessed December 20, 2008).
133. 'Implementation of the NPT Safeguards Agreement in the Islamic Republic of Iran', November 10, 2003, at http://www.iaea.org/Publications/Documents/Board/2003/gov2003-75.pdf, p. 8 (Accessed December 20, 2008); See also Rajesh Kumar Mishra, 'Iranian Nuclear Programme and Pakistan: Implications of the Linkages', *Strategic Analysis*, 28 (3), July-September 2004, pp. 440-453; Gordon Correra, *Shopping for bombs: Nuclear Proliferation, Global Insecurity and the Rise and Fall of the A.Q. Khan Network* (London: Hurst and Company, 2006, 2006), pp. 57-81.
134. R. Jeffrey Smith and Joby Warrick, 'Pakistani scientist Khan describes Iranian efforts to buy nuclear bombs', *The Washington Post*, March 14, 2010, at http://www.washingtonpost.com/wp-dyn/content/article/2010/03/13/AR2010031302258.html (Accessed December 20, 2008).
135. Kharazzi's reaction is available at 'World reaction to the Pakistani nuclear tests', at http://cns.miis.edu/archive/country_india/wreactpk.htm (Accessed December 20, 2008).
136. Cited in Christine Fair, 'India and Iran: New Delhi's balancing act', *The Washington Quarterly*, Summer 2007, Vol. 30, No. 3, p. 147; See also, K. Subrahmanyam, 'The case against Iran', *The Times of India*, November 21, 2005, at https://timesofindia.indiatimes.com/edit-page/the-case-against-iran/articleshow/1301822.cms (Accessed December 20, 2008).
137. K. Subrahmanyam, 'If Iran went nuclear' *The Indian Express*, October 5, 2005, at https://indianexpress.com/article/news-archive/if-iran-went-nuclear/ (Accessed December 20, 2008).
138. 'Indo-US N-deal to create new crisis: Iran', *The Economic Times*, October 5, 2008, at https://economictimes.indiatimes.com/news/politics-and-nation/indo-us-n-deal-to-create-new-crisis-iran/articleshow/3563135.cms?from=mdr (Accessed September 10, 2022).
139. The text of the Explanation of Vote at the IAEA is available at Rajya Sabha, 'Vote against Iran', December 17, 2009, at https://rsdebate.nic.in/bitstream/123456789/291324/1/IQ_218_17122009_U3122_p77_p78.pdf
140. Wikileaks, 'Cablegate: India Notes Us Iran Views; Trying to Clarify Its Position', September 9, 2005, at https://www.scoop.co.nz/stories/WL0509/S00012/cablegate-india-notes-us-iran-views-trying-to-clarify-its-position.htm (Accessed December 20, 2008).
141. C. Rajamohan, 'How the Iran nuke deal gives India room in the Greater Middle East', *The*

Indian Express, July 15, 2015, at https://indianexpress.com/article/explained/how-the-nuclear-deal-gives-india-room-in-the-greater-middle-east/ (Accessed July 20, 2015).

142. Ministry of External Affairs, 'Transcript of Media Briefing on Visit of PM of Israel to India by Secretary (ER)', January 15, 2018, at https://www.mea.gov.in/media-briefings.htm?dtl/29365 (Accessed January 16, 2018).
143. Ministry of Foreign Affairs, 'Response to terror attacks in Delhi and Tbilisi', February 13, 2012, at https://mfa.gov.il/mfa/pressroom/2012/pages/terror_attacks_delhi_tbilisi_13-feb-2012.aspx (Accessed April 20, 2012).
144. Ministry of External Affairs, 'Incident in New Delhi involving Israeli diplomat', March 16, 2012, at http://www.mea.gov.in/media-briefings.htm?dtl/19098/Incident+in+New+Delhi+involving+Israeli+diplomat (Accessed April 20, 2012); IANS, 'Israeli car blast: Red Corner notice issued against 4 Iranians', *India Today*, March 23, 2012, at https://www.indiatoday.in/india/north/story/embassy-car-bombing-interpol-red-corner-alert-iranians-96840-2012-03-23 (Accessed April 20, 2012).
145. Neeraj Chauhan, 'Delhi Police team draws blank in Iran', *The Times of India*, August 16, 2012, at http://timesofindia.indiatimes.com/articleshow/15509383.cms?utm_source=contentofinterest&utm_medium=text&utm_campaign=cppst (Accessed August 20, 2012).
146. Embassy of Israel in India, 'Two Years after the Attack on an Israeli Diplomat', February 13, 2014, at https://embassies.gov.il/delhi/NewsAndEvents/Pages/Two%20Years% 20After %20 the%20 Terror%20Attack %20on%20an%20Israeli%20Diplomat%20in%20New%20 Delhi.aspx (Accessed April 20, 2014).
147. T.V. Rajeswar, 'Cold War between Iran, Israel', *The Tribune*, March 5, 2012, at https://www.tribuneindia.com/2012/20120305/edit.htm#4 (Accessed April 20, 2012).
148. Saeed Kamali Dehghan, 'Iran nuclear scientist killed in Tehran motorbike bomb attack', *The Guardian*, January 11, 2012, at www.guardian.co.uk/world/2012/jan/11/iran-nuclear-scientist-killed (Accessed April 20, 2012).
149. 'Israeli embassy blast: Delhi court grants bail to four Kargil students', *The Hindu*, July 16, 2021, at https://www.thehindu.com/news/cities/Delhi/israeli-embassy-blast-delhi-court-grants-bail-to-four-arrested-from-ladakh/article35356040.ece (Accessed July 20, 2021).
150. Shishir Gupta, 'Iran guided Israeli embassy blast through local module, upsets India: Officials', *The Hindustan Times*, March 8, 2021, at https://www.hindustantimes.com/india-news/iran-guided-israeli-embassy-blast-through-local-module-upsets-india-officials-101615166916562.html (Accessed July 20, 2021).
151. Shubhajit Roy, 'Israel vs Iran, both take gloves off: Evil, childish, Pegasus, Zionist…', *The Indian Express*, November 2, 2021, at https://indianexpress.com/article/india/israel-vs-iran-naor-gilon-ambassador-to-india-7603359/ (Accessed November 20, 2021).
152. 'US Navy kills Indian fisherman in Persian Gulf', *DW*, July 17, 2012, at https://www.dw.com/en/us-navy-kills-indian-fisherman-in-persian-gulf/a-16101414 (Accessed July 20, 2021).

6

The Palestine De-Hyphenation

A significant feature of India's Israel policy under the Modi government is what has been termed as the 'de-hyphenation' of its policies with Israel vis-à-vis Palestine.[1] Just ahead of Prime Minister Modi's historic visit to Israel in July 2017, the Palestinian National Authority Chairman, President Mahmoud Abbas, visited India in May 2017. This was his fifth visit to the country. He had earlier visited India in May 2005, October 2008, February 2010 and September 2012. The 2015 visit, apart from the 2008 and 2012 visits, were State visits. In the Press Statement during Abbas's visit, Modi reiterated India's 'unwavering' support to the cause of Palestine, and expressed the hope that a 'sovereign, independent, united and viable Palestine, co-existing peacefully with Israel' will be realized.[2]

Analysts pointed out that the prime minister's statement differed from India's then extant policy positions on Palestine in bilateral and multilateral settings, in not explicitly stating that East Jerusalem will be the capital of a future Palestinian state. As was expected, Prime Minister Modi did not visit Palestine while visiting Israel in July 2017 but made a standalone visit to Ramallah in February 2018. This further strengthened the notion that India was following mutually beneficial policies with the two antagonists, without the bilateral interactions being impacted by its policies towards the other.

At the same time, it is pertinent to note that even if India has not reiterated the policy formulation of East Jerusalem as the capital of a Palestinian state in a bilateral setting, in multilateral settings, India has supported resolutions which explicitly state so. This is visible in the resolutions passed by the United Nations General Assembly (UNGA). In December 2021, for instance, India was among 156 countries that voted in favour of the resolution 'Permanent Sovereignty of the Palestinian people in the Occupied Palestinian Territory, including East Jerusalem, and of the Arab population in the occupied Syrian Golan over their natural resources'. Only seven countries—Canada, Federated States of Micronesia, Israel, Marshall Islands, Nauru, Palau and the US, voted against the resolution, while 15 countries abstained.[3]

The US, in an Explanation of its Vote, justifying its opposition to the resolution, termed it an 'unbalanced resolution that is unfairly critical of Israel, demonstrating a clear and persistent institutional bias directed at one member state' and affirmed that it 'will continue to oppose every effort to delegitimize Israel'.[4] It is significant that India continues to vote in favour of a resolution that Israel's closest ally, the US, views as an attempt to delegitimize it.

India's voting behaviour at forums like the UNGA, therefore, has been a point of contention between Indian and Israeli interlocutors. One of the first resolutions in a multilateral setting that the Modi government had to deal with after it assumed power was at the United Nations Human Rights Council (UNHRC) in July 2014, which voted to establish a Commission of Enquiry on Israel's military operation in the Gaza Strip, Operation Protective Edge, and investigate alleged human rights violations. A year later, India abstained on the resolution at the UNHRC which welcomed the report of the Commission of Enquiry. Israeli analysts saw this as a big change in India's positions.[5]

Others, though, rightly pointed out that the resolution related to the Hamas, which was designated as a terrorist organization by the US, among other nations, and that India continued to vote against Israel on most other resolutions. These include resolutions at the UNGA on the human rights situations in the Syrian Golan, the right to self-determination of the Palestinian people and resolutions criticizing Israeli settlement activities. India has expressed long-standing opposition to Israeli settlement activities, for instance, with Indian representatives at the UN calling them a 'stumbling block' and detrimental to the very premise of a two-state solution.[6]

In May 2021, India abstained in a vote at the same UNHRC on a resolution which called for an international investigation into human rights violations in the most recent Israeli military action in the Gaza Strip, Operation Guardian of the Walls. The Palestinian Foreign Minister Riad Malki is reported to have written to the Indian Foreign Minister S. Jaishankar criticizing the decision as one which 'stifled' the rights of the Palestinian people. The MEA Spokesperson, however, maintained that the Indian position was 'not new'.[7]

Earlier in October 2009, India had endorsed the Goldstone report, the fact-finding report of the enquiry commission led by South African jurist Richard Goldstone, on Israel's 2008-09 military operation in the Gaza Strip, Operation Cast Lead. Israel's Deputy Foreign Minister Danny Ayalon criticized the Indian decision as he contended that the Goldstone report denied 'the right of self-defence' to democracies'.[8] The report criticized both the Israeli government and Palestinian militant groups for their actions during the military confrontation.[9] In the special session of the UNGA in November 2009, the leader of the Indian delegation, Member of Parliament B.K. Hariprasad, though, stated that India had 'reservations' in making 'unqualified endorsement' of some the recommendations and procedures adopted by the Goldstone report…'. Hariprasad, at the same time, urged all concerned to take stern action against those responsible for human rights violations.[10]

The UN continues to an arena where India's policy positions on the Palestinian issue run counter to Israeli policy preferences. Among the significant Indian support to Palestinian-related resolutions at the UN have included the November 2012 resolution, which changed Palestine's status to that of a 'non-member observer'. Israel's military actions in the Gaza Strip, though, have been the main source of contention, in so far as they have generated pressures for the Indian government for appropriate responses. India has consistently maintained that it opposed rocket fire on Israeli civilian population centres, even as it has supported Israel's right to defend its people.

This was most evident in July 2014, when there was an unprecedented demand in the Indian Parliament for a resolution critical of Israel for its military action, Operation Protective Edge. The government countered by stating that no such demand was raised in the previous instances of military action in the Gaza Strip. Foreign Minister Sushma Swaraj even urged Rajya Sabha Chairman, Vice President Hamid Ansari not to allow the discussion on the conflict and subject as it refers 'discourteously to a friendly foreign country'.[11]

The debate, though, eventually took place in the Rajya Sabha on July 21, with twenty Members of Parliament taking part in the discussion, with three-fourths of them belonging to regional and communist parties. The other five belonged to the ruling Bharatiya Janata Party (BJP) and the Indian National Congress (INC). Members belonging to the regional parties pointed out that no such demand for a critical resolution was aired against Sri Lanka, for instance, for its treatment of the Tamil minorities. Only two members, Asaduddin Owaisi of the All India Majlis Ittehadul Muslimeen (AIMIM) and Sitaram Yechury of the Communist Party of India-Marxist (CPI-M), called for an end to the defence relationship with Israel.

Foreign Minister Sushma Swaraj, in her remarks, asked the Parliament not to politicize the country's response to the Gaza Conflict and reiterated the government's stand that it continued to support the Palestinian cause 'wholeheartedly' even as it will continue to strengthen the country's relations with Israel. Interestingly, Member of Parliament Tarun Vijay of the BJP, reminded the members that India cannot be seen to be 'more Arab than the Arabs', in their support for the Palestinian cause. He made this remark in the light of the fact that Israel was fighting the Hamas, a militant organization that was shunned by the Arab world itself.[12] His comments also shine light on the fact that the Palestinian issue has been relegated lower down in the list of Arab priorities, given their own domestic socio-economic churning and regional strategic dynamics.

This has been especially so in the aftermath of the Arab Spring and more so, after the Abraham Accords. The fact that the UAE and countries like Morocco, later, established full diplomatic ties with Israel in August 2020, despite the 2002 Arab Consensus, which mandated that full ties would only be established with the Jewish state after the formation of the Palestinian state, is reflective of the changed regional consensus. Israel's Ambassador to India,

Naor Gilon, while speaking at the Manohar Parrikar Institute for Defence Studies and Analyses (MP-IDSA) on September 21, 2022, acknowledged that the Modi government's successful compartmentalization of its Palestine and Israel polices was an inspiration and example for Gulf countries to take similar policy positions and pursue overt, beneficial relations with Israel.

Saudi Arabia and its regional allies, though, continue to view the Islamic Republic's regional policies with apprehension. Iran and the Saudi-led camps are pitted against each other in regional hotspots, ranging from Yemen to Syria. The Iranian nuclear contentions, meanwhile, have been exacerbated in the aftermath of the 2018 withdrawal from the JCPOA by the Trump administration. Groups like the Hamas, with which Israel has been having violent conflicts in the Gaza Strip, are also viewed with concern by countries like Saudi Arabia, given that it is seen as an offshoot of the Muslim Brotherhood, which poses a domestic concern in some of these countries.

India's developmental and political support to the Palestinians, meanwhile, has continued and increased. Apart from Prime Minister Modi in February 2018, President Pranab Mukherjee and Foreign Minister Sushma Swaraj visited Ramallah in October 2015 and January 2016, respectively. During Modi's visit in February 2018, he became the first world leader to visit the newly constructed mausoleum of Yasser Arafat. President Mukherjee emphasized that 'India's empathy with the Palestinian cause and its friendship with the people of Palestine have become an integral part of our foreign policy'.[13] Even as the Modi government refused to support an anti-Israel resolution in Parliament in July 2014, it reiterated the governments' continued support to the Palestinian cause.

As for developmental support, India gave $27 million in grants to the Palestinians, till 2008.[14] India's annual contribution to the United Nations Reliefs and Works Agency (UNRWA) was increased from $200,000 to $1 million, in 2009. This was later increased to $1.5 million, and subsequently to $5 million in 2018—in the light of the Trump administration's decision to stop funding to the Agency. Nearly $60 million of grant projects were being implemented in September 2020.[15] Major projects that India has helped build include schools, vocational training centres, and technology parks.

India also continues to urge both the antagonists to work towards establishing the two-state solution. Foreign Secretary Harsh Vardhan Shringla, at the United Nations Security Council (UNSC) meeting on the Middle East peace process in August 2021, reiterated this core position.[16] The possibility of this core principle being realized, though, is shrinking, due to continued intransigence by both sides and unwillingness to come to a compromise on core issues relating to borders, status of Jerusalem, refuges, among others.

Public opinion polls, though, as conducted by the Israel Democracy Institute, for instance, show that while the percentage of those who support a two-state solution has reduced over the years—from around 70 per cent in 2007 to 40 per cent currently, the option of a two-state solution still garnered the most votes as an optimum solution to the intractable conflict, among the polled Israeli public.[17] A June 2021 poll by the Palestinian Center for Policy and Survey Research—conducted after the latest round of fighting in the Gaza Strip with the Israelis, found that 39 per cent of Palestinians still supported the two-state solution, down from 71 per cent in 2006.[18] Israeli analysts also note that the two-state solution was still Israel's best option, to reserve the Jewish majority status of the State of Israel.[19]

NOTES

1. P.R. Kumaraswamy, 'Modi Redefines India's Palestine Policy', *MPIDSA Issue Brief*, May 18, 2017, at https://www.idsa.in/issuebrief/modi-redefines-india-palestine-policy_prkumaraswamy _180517 (Accessed January 5, 2022).
2. Ministry of External Affairs, 'Press Statement by Prime Minister during the State Visit of President of Palestine to India', May 16, 2017, at http://mea.gov.in/Speeches-Statements.htm?dtl/28466/Press_Statement_by_Prime_Minister_during_the_State_Visit_of_ President_of_ Palestine_to_India_May_16_2017 (Accessed January 5, 2022).
3. The text of the resolution is available at https://documents-dds-ny.un.org/doc/UNDOC/GEN/ N21/371/59/PDF/N2137159.pdf?OpenElement (Accessed January 5, 2022).
4. United States Mission to the United Nations, 'Explanation of Vote for the Second Committee Adoption of the Permanent Sovereignty of the Palestinian People in the Occupied Palestinian Territory', November 18, 2021, at https://usun.usmission.gov/explanation-of-vote-for-the-second-committee-adoption-of-the-permanent-sovereignty-of-the-palestinian-people-in-the-occupied-palestinian-territory/ (Accessed June 10, 2022).
5. Herb Keinon, 'Diplomacy: Shifts happen, India and the Israeli-Palestinian conflict', *The Jerusalem Post*, July 10 2015, at https://www.jpost.com/international/diplomacy-shifts-happen-india-and-the-israeli-palestinian-conflict-408559 (Accessed January 5, 2022); See also Herb Keinon, 'As PA expresses "shock" at India's UN vote, Israel voices appreciation for abstention', *The Jerusalem Post*, July 7, 2015, at https://www.jpost.com/israel-news/politics-and-diplomacy/

as-pa-expresses-shock-at-indias-un-vote-israel-voices-appreciation-for-abstention-408287 (Accessed January 5, 2022).

6. See United Nations General Assembly, 'Adopting Six Resolutions by Recorded Vote, General Assembly Concludes Annual Debates on Question of Palestine, Wider Middle East Situation', November 30, 2012, at https://press.un.org/en/2012/ga11319.doc.htm (Accessed January 5, 2022); This was incidentally, India's then Permanent Representative at the UN, Hardeep Singh Puri, currently India's Minister for Petroleum and Natural Gas.
7. 'Stand at U.N. Human Rights Council on Palestine not new: India', *The Hindu*, June 3, 2021, at https://www.thehindu.com/news/national/stand-at-un-human-rights-council-on-palestine-not-new-india/article34721755.ece (Accessed January 5, 2022).
8. Ministry of Foreign Affairs, 'Dep FM Ayalon comments on Human Rights Council vote', October 17, 2009, http://www.mfa.gov.il/MFA/About+the+Ministry/MFA+Spokesman/2009/Press+releases/Dep_FM_Ayalon_comments_Human_Rights_Council_vote_17-Oct-2009 (Accessed September 15, 2011).
9. See United Nations Human Rights Council, 'Human Rights in Palestine and Other Occupied Arab Territories', September 15, 2009, at https://www.un.org/ruleoflaw/files/UNFFMGC_Report.pdf (Accessed September 15, 2011).
10. See Press Trust of India, 'India votes in favour of Goldstone report', *The Economic Times*, November 6, 2009, at https://economictimes.indiatimes.com/news/politics-and-nation/india-votes-in-favour-of-goldstone-report/articleshow/5201952.cms?from=mdr (Accessed September 15, 2011).
11. See Rajya Sabha, 'Uncorrected verbatim debates', Session No. 232, July 17, 2014, at https://rajyasabha.nic.in/business/newshow.aspx (Accessed August 10, 2014).
12. See Rajya Sabha, 'Uncorrected verbatim debates', Session No. 232, July 21, 2014, at https://rajyasabha.nic.in/business/newshow.aspx (Accessed August 10, 2014).
13. Press Information Bureau, 'Speech by the President of India, Shri Pranab Mukherjee in response to President Abbas' remarks at the state Banquet', October 12, 2015, at http://pib.nic.in/newsite/PrintRelease.aspx?relid=128665 (Accessed October 15, 2015).
14. Ministry of External Affairs, 'Statement by Ambassador of India to Indonesia and Head of Delegation Mr. Biren Nanda at the New Asia-Africa Strategic Partnership Ministerial Conference on Capacity Building for Palestine (NAASP) in Jakarta', July 14, 2008, at https://www.mea.gov.in/incoming-visit-detail-hi.htm?1574/Statement+by+Mr+Biren+Nanda+Ambassador+of+ India+to+Indonesia+ and+Head+of+Delegation+at+N ew+AsiaAfrica+Strategic + Partnership+Ministerial+ Conference+on+Capacity+Building+ for+ Palestine+ at+Jakarta (Accessed September 15, 2011).
15. Ministry of External Affairs, '3rd Round of India-Palestine Foreign Office Consultations', September 10, 2020, at http://mea.gov.in/press-releases.htm?dtl/32955/3rd+round+of+indiapalestine+foreign+office+consultations (Accessed September 30, 2021).
16. Ministry of External Affairs, 'Statement by Foreign Secretary at UNSC meeting on the Middle East Peace Process, including the Palestine Question', August 30, 2021, at http://mea.gov.in/Speeches-Statements.htm?dtl/34207/statement+by+foreign+secretary+at+unsc+meeting+on+the+ middle+east+peace+process+including+the+palestine+question (Accessed September 30, 2021).
17. Tovah Lazaroff, 'With only 40 per cent support, Israelis still think 2 states best option: poll', *The Jerusalem Post*, August 4, 2021, at https://www.jpost.com/arab-israeli-conflict/with-only-40-percent-support-israelis-still-think-2-states-best-option-poll-675838 (Accessed September 30, 2021).

18. Dina Smeltz and Emily Sullivan, 'Americans Favor a Two-State Solution More Than Israelis and Palestinians Do', July 9, 2021, at https://www.thechicagocouncil.org/commentary-and-analysis/blogs/americans-favor-two-state-solution-more-israelis-and-palestinians-do (Accessed September 30, 2021).
19. Emily Schrader, 'Two-state solution still is Israel's only option: opinion', *The Jerusalem Post,* December 20, 2021, at https://www.jpost.com/opinion/article-689281 (Accessed January 20, 2022).

7

Going Forward

Even as the India-Israel defence partnership is set to grow and solidify in the coming future, India's defence self-reliance drive will impact, to an extent, the quantum of the relationship. India's defence modernization needs are huge, as well as the need to effectively meet the growing security concerns across the internal and external spectrum. The all-encompassing Pakistan-China defence cooperation, which equips Islamabad with sophisticated equipment and platforms, is too stark to be ignored for India's security planners.

As seen in the above sections, India and Israel have developed an all-round defence and security partnership, with increasing focus on joint development and production. Exports of Indian-manufactured Israeli equipment like UAVs to countries in Southeast Asia is taking place, and both sides can further explore similar arenas of cooperation where the two countries could focus their efforts, especially by the private sector companies. Joint ventures in the category of small arms and ammunition, for instance, have big plans not just to supply to the requirements of the India armed forces but also to export markets.

India's defence relationship with Israel is being sought to be leveraged to improve the country's defence exports profile. The electronics major, BEL, for instance, has expressed an interest in having a tie up with the IAI to boost the DPSU's exports profile. Way back in 2003, HAL had a tie-up with the IAI to market the Advanced Light Helicopter (ALH). The country's central public sector enterprises (CPSE) were tasked by Prime Minister Modi in 2018 to ensure that at least 25 per cent of their revenue should be from exports by 2022-23. It remains to be seen how the two entities can pursue this further. The IAI has a well-established international profile and marketing prowess, an element that Indian DPSUs as well as private sector companies can study and take advantage of.

A critical arena of focus has to invariably be the effort to produce cutting-edge equipment, which can also stand the test of quality and reliability. The plethora of steps taken by the MoD in recent past are expected to make the Indian defence eco-system more vibrant and dynamic. Such an eco-system will no doubt, going forward, help in realizing the country's indigenization as well as domestic manufacturing and export targets. As noted in Chapter Two, a strengthened Indian defence industrial eco-system, coupled with measures like the Srijan defence indigenization portal, could cumulatively reduce the volume and quantum of defence imports from partners like Israel.

Given the extraordinary range of cooperation in terms of procurement and joint development of equipment ranging from missiles like LRSAM, MRSAM, radars, UAVs, assault weapons, among others, we may not see an immediate drastic reduction of the quantum of the India-Israel defence trade, in the immediate to short term. The Israeli defence industry is also well placed—given its long-standing exposure to the Indian market, to take advantage of the government's various measures to help in domestic manufacturing. These include relaxed norms for foreign direct investment (FDI), in case the foreign OEMs agree to transfer of technology.

Going forward, as and when India's indigenous capabilities in areas like AWACS or UAVs mature, dependence on foreign suppliers can be expected to reduce. India's big indigenization focus in critical areas of aero engine, materials and electronic chip technology is expected to only witness higher volumes of procurement from indigenous sources—including niche equipment like AEW&C aircraft, AESA radars, among other equipment. These are the kinds of equipment that India has imported from Israel.

Domestic procurement of such equipment, therefore, will result in concurrently lesser quantum of imports from strategic partners like Israel.

Even if Indian capabilities come up to speed in areas where there are deficiencies, it is also a fact that it is not economically viable or strategically prudent to build each and every weapon system in a country's defence inventory indigenously. Israeli defence industry strengths in such niche technological areas can continue to act as 'force multipliers' and add critical value to India's defence inventory.

India's defence market is one of the biggest in the world and there is space and scope for cooperation with critical strategic partners like Israel to continue to grow to fulfill the varied requirements of the Indian armed forces. India expects to spend significantly on defence modernization in the near future. Strategic partners like Israel, even as they continue to occupy an important place in fulfilling the modernization and upgradation requirements of India's armed forces, will be expected to continue to work more closely with the domestic defence industry—both the defence public sector units and the private sector, to fulfill the critical requirements of India's armed forces.

As for border/internal security cooperation, Chapter Three has delineated in brief the formidable reputation that Israel has built regarding its counter-terror and border security tactics. The Israeli experience has proved to be successful in mitigating the loss of Israeli lives. Israel follows a range of tactics, including military responses to rocket strikes and targeted killings. The country swears by the importance and efficacy of such tactics. India has indeed benefited from closely reading the Israeli experience as well as trying to emulate its technological solutions, especially with regard to border security.

India's border guarding forces, while acknowledging the importance of learning best practices from around the world, flag the enormous complexities involved in securing thousands of kilometres of the country's borders. It is also acknowledged that the sources of threat are different for both the countries, as indeed the nature of the sanctuary, in the form of safe havens, provided by Pakistan, as against Israel—which largely faces Palestinian terrorism and the Hezbollah, which is a significant domestic political force in Israel's neighbouring country, Lebanon. While Israel accuses Iran of supplying the Hezbollah and Gaza militants with rockets and financial resources to target it, the long-standing and wide-ranging institutional as well as direct support to jihadist elements to wage war against India has been far more insidious.

Israel's long history of using punitive military strikes to take out enemy capabilities before they can cause damage is another feature closely studied around the world. Israel, in recent times, has launched air strikes in places as far away as Iraq, on the basis of its well-endowed intelligence capabilities that inimical actors supported by countries like Iran were using that territory to process weapons and ammunition targeted against it.

In August 2019, for instance, Israel launched air strikes against alleged weapons depots in Iraq, being used by Iran to supply weapons to armed groups like the Hezbollah in Syria. India's Balakot strike, where specialized Israeli weapons systems were used, has led analysts to opine that India too was following Israeli tactics to respond to blatant aggression on its territory by militants supported by Pakistan. India can continue to benefit from the Israeli experience of using active defence measures, punitive strikes, perimeter security solutions, targeted killings, among a range of choices, to ensure the security and well-being of its people.

On the Iranian nuclear issue, India has adopted positions largely in opposition to the preferred Israeli policy preferences, vis-à-vis the optimum manner in which to address the nuclear contentions. India has also actively defended the role of the IAEA, and has urged that the nuclear regulatory authority's role be given prime importance in the efficient discharge of its duties. The India-Iran trade and energy security relationship has been severely impacted as a result of the US policy positions on the Iran nuclear imbroglio, both prior to the signing of the JCPOA and after the Trump withdrawal.

India has also made it clear from the beginning that it was opposed to the possibility of a nuclear Iran, given the negative repercussions for regional security and stability as well as due to the Iran-Pakistan/A.Q. Khan proliferation linkages. India also actively pursued its Iran policy keeping in mind its larger regional interests relating to connectivity. These efforts, however, came under pressure due to the uncertainties surrounding the Iranian nuclear programme and administration-contingent US foreign policies on multilaterally negotiated agreements like the JCPOA. The Chahbahar port, apart from energy security considerations—including the issue of Indian investments in Iranian energy infrastructure, faced headwinds. While the Shahid Behesti terminal is still being run by the IPGL, Indian officials have reiterated the importance of the port for Afghanistan and have highlighted the connectivity advantages the port can offer to Central Asian countries.

In the aftermath of the signing of the Abraham Accords between Israel and the UAE in August 2020, meanwhile, the regional geo-strategic divide has gained an added definition, more clearly marking the rival camps. The first meeting of the West Asian Quad—when Foreign Minister Jaishankar was in Israel in October 2021, signified the making of a new and potent regional grouping, with the potential to usher in new vistas of development cooperation. As in the case of the East Asian Quad, it remains to be seen the extent to which the West Asian Quad members engage with each other on issues of regional security and stability.

The first ever I2U2 Summit meeting between the leaders of India, Israel, the UAE and the US, when President Biden visited Israel in July 2022, clearly indicates the geo-economic focus of the unique mini-lateral made up of critical nation states of South Asia, West Asia and the US. The focus areas of cooperation, as noted in earlier sections, relate to water, energy, transportation, space, health and food security, with cooperative projects relating to food security set in motion.

As of now, the I2U2 are therefore confining themselves to areas of developmental cooperation. India will be expected to jealously guard her independent foreign policy, guided by national interests and the interests of its vast regional diaspora. It is difficult to see India being actively part of a regional military undertaking/alliance structure whose sole aim will be to contain Iran. To that extent, India's policy positions could continue to pit her against the policy preferences of a close strategic partner like Israel. This despite India and Israel sharing the same objectives vis-à-vis the Iranian nuclear programme, even as both sides differ on the process to achieve those objectives—with Israel continuing to privilege muscular solutions to set back the Iranian capabilities.

That being said, India's overt identification with the West Asian Quad members—Israel, the UAE and the US, is in contrast to Iran's increasingly close partnership with China—a growing major power opposed to the US's and India's regional role. Iran and China signed a 25-year strategic partnership agreement in March 2021. Iran's Foreign Minister Amir Abdollahian, while visiting Beijing in January 2022, stated that the agreement was being implemented. Reports note that the agreement envisages Chinese investments of over $400 billion in Iranian infrastructure projects, among other areas of cooperation.

During the visit of President Xi Jinping to Tehran in 2016, both sides had set an expansive target of $600 billion of bilateral trade to be achieved by 2026. Bilateral trade between the countries was around $23 billion in 2019, up from $10 billion in 2005. During January-December 2021, though, it was around $15 billion.[1] Xi's 2016 visit was in the aftermath of the beginning of implementation of the JCPOA (in January 2016), which led to sanctions relief, among other economic benefits for Iran. After the Trump withdrawal, however, even as reports note that China is continuing to import significant quantities of Iranian oil, the volume of bilateral trade has reduced.

Apart from economic interactions, reports note expanding military cooperation between the two countries. Chinese Defence Minister Wei Fenghe visited Tehran in April 2022, with both sides pledging to expand cooperation. China, Iran, along with Russia, held a trilateral naval drill in the northern Indian Ocean in January 2022, the third time the three navies met since 2019. Iran signed a MoU to join the Shanghai Cooperation Organisation (SCO) in September 2022. While China has mostly supplied anti-ship missiles to Iran in the past two decades, in the aftermath of the expiry of the UN conventional arms embargo in October 2020 (imposed in 2010), Iran-China arms trade can also be expected to increase. Around 20 per cent of Iran's arms imports were sourced from China (as per SIPRI Trend Indicator Values), as against 60 per cent from Russia, during 2000-21.[2] Apart from the Iran-China dynamics, Beijing is also rapidly expanding its Indian Ocean and Persian Gulf naval footprints.

India's regional choices and opportunities, therefore, for the foreseeable future, seem increasingly to lie in benefiting from greater collaboration with the West Asian Quad members. India's organic linkages with the region, robust and expanding bilateral interactions, the country's diaspora, energy linkages and increasing participation of West Asian states in India's growth story, will hold it in good stead as New Delhi navigates near to mid-term headwinds flowing out of the US-Iran and Israel-Iran conflictual dynamics.

India's Palestine policy, meanwhile, will continue to be guided by its core principles on the issue, even as the possibility of an independent Palestinian state, living side by side with Israel, looks difficult to materialize in the near to mid-terms. This, even as the schisms within the Palestinian national movement, look set to expand in the post-Mahmoud Abbas era.

India-Israel relations, therefore, have traversed a dynamic path in the past three decades and have attained a higher orbit, after the coming to power of the Modi government. Bilateral relations have been strengthened, in areas of defence, developmental and high-technology cooperation. New vistas of cooperation can be expected to be exploited by both the sides, to expand the scope of cooperation to involve third countries—including in West Asia specifically, as well as in Southeast Asia and/or Africa. India and Israel, for instance, have robust developmental partnership programs with many countries in Africa. An India-Israel enhanced strategic partnership, can be a win-win proposition, bilaterally and across regions.

NOTES

1. 'Iran-China trade reaches $14.8b in 2021', *Tehran Times*, February 5, 2022, at https://www.tehrantimes.com/news/469820/Iran-China-trade-reaches-14-8b-in-2021 (Accessed July 20, 2022).
2. SIPRI, 'TIV of arms exports to Iran, 2000-2021', Importer-Exporter TIV Tables, at https://armstrade.sipri.org/armstrade/page/values.php (Accessed July 22, 2022).

APPENDIX

Table 1: India-Israel Memorandum of Understandings (2014-2022)

Subject	*Ministries/Institutions Involved*	*When signed*
Economic	Double taxation avoidance agreement	October 2015
	Memorandum of Intent between Invest India and Invest in Israel	January 2018
Culture	Cultural exchange programme, for years 2015-18	October 2015
Education	JNU-BGU	October 2015
	Hebrew University and IIT (Kharagpur)	October 2015
	IIT (Kharagpur) and Ben Gurion University	October 2015
	JNU and Hebrew University	October 2015
	IIT (Kharagpur) and University of Haifa	October 2015
	University of Delhi and Ben Gurion University	October 2015
	Hebrew University and University of Delhi	October 2015
	University of Delhi and IDC, Herzliya	October 2015
Science and Technology	India-Israel Industrial R&D and Technological Innovation Fund (I4F)	July 2017
	Letter of Intent between Indian Oil Cooperation Limited (IOCL) and Phinergy Ltd. for cooperation in the area of metal-air batteries	January 2018
	Letter of Intent between IOCL and Yeda Research and Development Co Ltd for cooperation in the area of concentrated solar thermal technologies	January 2018
Bilateral Framework	Strategic Partnership; Strategic Partnership in Water and Agriculture	July 2017
Water	National Campaign for Water Conservation in India	July 2017
	State Water Utility Reform in India, Uttar Pradesh	July 2017
Agriculture	Declaration of Intent Between the Ministry of Agriculture and Rural Development of the State of Israel and the Ministry ofAgriculture of the Republic of India	November 2016

Subject	*Ministries/Institutions Involved*	*When signed*
	Three Year Work Program in Agriculture 2018-2020	July 2017
Space	Plan of Cooperation Between ISRO and the ISA regarding cooperation in Atomic Clocks	July 2017
	MoU between the ISRO and ISA regarding cooperation in GEO-LEO Optical Link	July 2017
	MoU between ISRO and ISA regarding cooperation in Electric Propulsion for Small Satellites	July 2017
	MoU between Indian Institute of Space Science and Technology (IIST) and the Technion-Israel Institute of Technology	January 2018
	Plan of Cooperation between ISRO and ISA regarding cooperation in Electric Propulsion for Small Satellites	April 2020
Cyber security	To develop, promote and expand cooperation in the field of HRD through training programmes, skill development, and simulator based hands-on training	January 2018
	MoU between the computer emergency response team (CERT) of India and Israel	July 2020
Oil and Gas sector	MoU between Indian Ministry of Petroleum and Natural Gas and Israeli Ministry of Energy	January 2018
Air transport	Protocol on Amendments to the Air Transport Agreement (on issues like code sharing etc.)	January 2018
Film production	Agreement on Film-co-production, to further develop cultural ties	January 2018
Homeopathic Medicine	MoU between the Central Council for Research in Homeopathy, Ministry of AYUSH and the Centre for Integrative Complementary Medicine, Shaare Zedek Medical Center	January 2018
Defence	Bilateral innovation agreement between DRDO and Israel's Directorate of Defence Research and Development (DDR&D)	2021

Source: Ministry of External Affairs, www.mea.gov.in (Accessed January 30, 2022).

Table 2: India-Palestine Memorandum of Understandings (2014-2022)

Subject	*Ministries/Institutions Involved*	*When signed*
Cultural Relations	MOU between Indian Council for Cultural Relations (ICCR) and Ministry of Culture, State of Palestine	October 2015
Information Technology	MoU on Palestine-India Techno Park, Ramallah	October 2016
Diplomatic	MoU on Visa Exemption on Diplomatic and Official Passports	May 2017
Youth Affairs and Sports	MoU on Cooperation in Youth Affairs and Sports	May 2017
Economic	National printing press, Ramallah	February 2018
Agriculture	MoU on Agricultural Cooperation	May 2017
	MoU on Information-Technology and Electronics	May 2017
Healthcare	MoU on Cooperation in Health Sector	May 2017
	India-Palestine Super-Speciality Hospital, Beit Shahour	February 2018
Social Welfare	India-Palestine Centre for Empowering Women	February 2018
Education	MOU between Jawaharlal Nehru University (JNU) and Birziet University	October 2015
	MOU between JNU and Al Najah National University	October 2015
	MOU between Jamia Milia Islamia and Al Quds University	October 2015
	MOU between Jamia Milia Islamia and Al Istiklal University	October 2015
	MOU between Jamia Milia Islamia and Hebron University	October 2015
	School at Muthalth Al Shuhada Village	February 2018
	School at Tamoon village in Tubas Governorate	February 2018
	Additional floor in Jawaharlal Nehru School for Boys	February 2018

Source: Ministry of External Affairs, www.mea.gov.in (Accessed January 30, 2022).

Table 3: India-Israel Defence Procurement Deals (2014-2022)

Equipment	*Signed/Procured/Delivered/Deployed*
Barak-I missiles	2014
SPICE smart bombs	2015
Tadiran combat radios	2016
Barak-I missiles	2017
Spyder Low Level Quick Reaction Missile (LLQRM) system	2017
Heron TP UAVs	2018
Spike ATGMs SPICE smart bombs	2019
Negev NG-7 LMG Spike ATGMs SPICE smart bombs	2020
Sky Striker drones Heron Medium Altitude Long Endurance (MALE) UAVs Masada pistols	2021

Source: Press Information Bureau, www.pib.nic.in (Accessed January 30, 2022); Media reports

Table 4: India-Israel Joint Development Programmes (Missiles)

Weapons System	*MoU signed*	*Weapon Inducted*	*Partners*
LRSAM(Navy)	2006	Feb 2021	Bharat Electronics Limited (BEL); Israel Aerospace Industries (IAI); DRDO; Rafael; Larsen and Toubro
MRSAM (Air Force)	2009	Sept 2021	
MRSAM (Army)	2017	Successful maiden launch conducted in December 2020	

Source: Ministry of Defence, Annual Reports, www.mod.nic.in (Accessed January 30, 2022)

Table 5: India-Israel Defence Joint Ventures

Indian partner	*Israeli partner*	*Contracts executed/ Being Executed/ JVs formed to Explore Opportunities*
HAL	IAI	Boeing passenger jets to conversion to cargo aircraft
		Gulf Stream G-50 Fuselage
		Boeing main deck cargo doors
HAL	Elbit Systems-ISTAR Division	VTOL UAVs
HAL	Elbit Systems	Digital head up displays
HAL, Dynamatic Technologies	IAI	UAVs
Tatas	Elta Systems Limited	EW; Homeland security
Adani Defence and Aerospace; Alpha Design Technologies Pvt Ltd.	Elbit Systems	UAVs
Kalyani Group, Larsen and Toubro (along with Bharat Dynamics Limited and Bharat Electronics Limited)	Rafael Advanced Systems	MRSAM missile kits
PLR Systems (Adani Grp has a stake)	Israel Weapons Industries (IWI)	Small arms and ammunition
HBL Power Systems	Elta Systems	Radar technology
Tatas	Israel Aerospace Industries (IAI)	Radar applications
Alpha Design	Elbit Security Systems	Sky Striker UAVs
		Mi-17 helicopter upgrades
Wipro	Israel Aerospace Industries	Composite aero structures
Mahindra Aerostructure	Elbit Systems-Cyclone	Aerostructures
Dynamatic Technologies Private Limited and Elcom	Israel Aerospace Industries (IAI)	UAVs
Kalyani Strategic Systems Limited	Israel Aerospace Industries (IAI)	Air defence systems, radars, among other opportunities
Mahindra Telephonics	Shachaf Engineering	Strategic Electronics
Bharat Forge	Elbit Systems	Artillery systems

Source: Media reports, Company statements

Table 6: Port Visits of Indian Naval Ships to Haifa

INS Mysore INS Godavari INS Ganga INS Shakti	Guided missile destroyer Guided missile frigate Guided missile frigate Fleet tanker	2004
INS Mumbai INS Brahmaputra	Guided missile destroyer Guided missile frigate	June 2006
INS Mumbai INS Trishul INS Gomti INS Aditya	Guided missile destroyer Stealth missile frigate Guided missile frigate Tanker	August 2012
INS Trikhand	Frigate	August 2015
INS Mumbai INS Trishul INS Aditya	Guided missile Destroyer Stealth missile frigate Tanker	May 2017
INS Tarangini	Sail training ship	September 2018

Source: Ministry of Defence, Annual Reports, www.mod.nic.in; Ministry of External Affairs, Annual Reports, www.mea.gov.in, Media reports, Press Information Bureau, www.pib.nic.in (Accessed January 25, 2022)

Table 7: Key Institutional Interactions (2014-2022)

Area	*Framework/Participants*	*When*
Coastal Security	Indian Coast Guard and Israeli Navy	July 2018
Homeland/Internal/ Border Security	1st Joint Steering Committee meeting between India andIsrael on HLS cooperation	September 2014
	2nd Joint Steering Committee meeting between India andIsrael on HLS cooperation	February 2018
	4th meeting of JWG on border management	November 2018
	3rd Joint Steering Committee meeting between India andIsrael on HLS cooperation	January 2020
	14th JWG meeting on counter-terrorism	February 2020
Defence	11th JWG on defence	June 2014
	14th JWG on defence	July 2018
	15th JWG on defence	October 2021
	Staff Talks (Army, Navy, Airforce)	Annual
Foreign Ministry	Foreign Office consultations	Annual

Source: Ministry of Defence, Annual Reports, www.mod.nic.in; Ministry of External Affairs, Annual Reports, www.mea.gov.in, Ministry of Home Affairs, Annual Reports, www.mha.gov.in; Media reports, Press Information Bureau, www.pib.nic.in (Accessed January 25, 2022)

Table 8: Visits of Service Chiefs (2014-2022)

		Army	*Navy*	*Air Force*
India	2014	Gen. Bikram Singh		
	2016			Air Chief Marshal Arup Raha
	2017		Adm. Sunil Lanba	
	2018			Air Chief Marshal Birender Singh Dhanoa
	2021	Gen. M.M. Naravane		Air Chief Marshal R.S. Bhadauria
Israel	2015		Adm. Ram Rutberg	Maj. Gen. Amir Eshel, Commander of Israeli Air and Space Forces
	2017	Maj. Gen. Herzi Halevi, Chief of Defence Intelligence and Chief of Ground Forces, Maj. Gen. Kobi Barak		
	2019			Maj. Gen. Amikam Norkin, Commander of Israel Air Force (March 2019)
				Maj. Gen. Amikam Norkin, Commander of Israel Air Force (August 2019)

Source: Media reports; Ministry of Defence, www.mod.nic.in; Ministry of External Affairs, Annual Reports, www.mea.gov.in (Accessed January 25, 2022).

Table 9: High-Level Visits (2014-22)

Year	*India*	*Israel*
2014	Rajnath Singh, Union Minister for Home Affairs	
2015	Devendra Fadnavis, Maharashtra Chief Minister	Agriculture Minister Yair Shamir
	President Pranab Mukherjee to Israel and Palestine	Defence Minister Moshe Yaa'lon
2016	External Affairs Minister Sushma Swaraj	Agriculture Minister Uri Ariel
	Radha Mohan Singh, Union Minister for Agriculture	President Reuven Rivlin
	Prakash Javadekar, Union Minister for Human Resources Development	Space, Science and Technology Minister Ofir Akunis
2017	First All-Party Parliamentary Delegation	Agriculture Minister Uri Ariel
	Prime Minister Narendra Modi	
2018	Manohar Lal Khattar, Chief Minister of Haryana	Prime Minister Benjamin Netanyahu
	Subodh Uniyal, Uttrakhand Agriculture Minister	
	Pandurang Fundkar, Maharashtra Agriculture Minister	
	Purushotam Rupala, Minister of State for Agriculture	
	Vijay Rupani, Gujarat Chief Minister	
	Amarinder Singh, Punjab Chief Minister	
2019	Gajendra Singh Shekhawat, Union Minister for Jal Shakti	
2021	External Affairs Minister S. Jaishankar Prime Minister Modi met Israeli Prime Minister Naftali Bennet, Glasgow (Sidelines of COP 22 climate summit)	
2022	Narendra Singh Tomar, Minister of Agriculture and Farmer's Welfare	

Source: Media reports; Ministry of Defence, www.mod.nic.in; Ministry of External Affairs, Annual Reports, www.mea.gov.in (Accessed May 15, 2022)

Table 10: India-Israel Bilateral Trade 2012-22

(In USD Million)

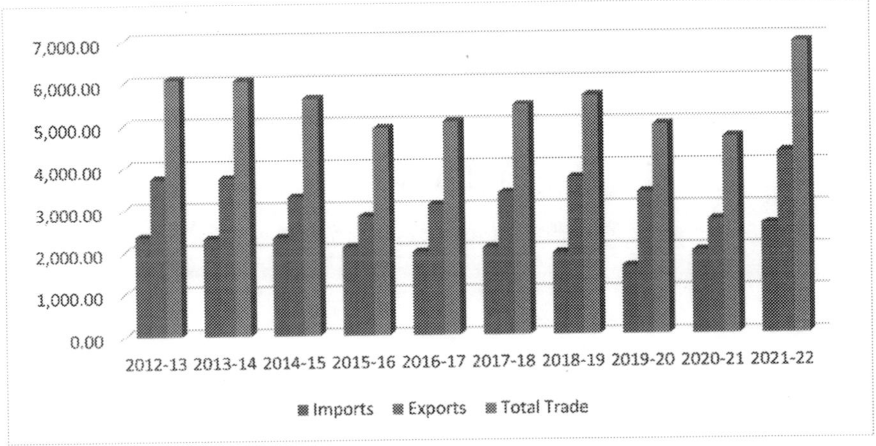

Source: Ministry of Commerce and Industry, 'Export Import Data Bank', at https://tradestat.commerce.gov.in/eidb/default.asp (Accessed July 10, 2022).

INDEX

*